Working with Student Teachers

Getting and Giving the Best

Second Edition

Michael A. Morehead, Lawrence Lyman,
and Harvey C. Foyle

Rowman & Littlefield Education
Lanham • New York • Toronto • Plymouth, UK

b3163 1812

Published in the United States of America
by Rowman & Littlefield Education
A Division of Rowman & Littlefield Publishers, Inc.
A wholly owned subsidary of The Rowman & Littlefield Publishing Group, Inc.
4501 Forbes Boulevard, Suite 200, Lanham, Maryland 20706
www.rowmaneducation.com

Estover Road
Plymouth PL6 7PY
United Kingdom

British Library Cataloguing in Publication Information Available

Library of Congress Cataloging-in-Publication Data

Morehead, Michael A.
  Working with student teachers : getting and giving the best / Michael A.
Morehead, Lawrence Lyman, and Harvey C. Foyle. — 2nd ed.
      p. cm.
  Includes bibliographical references.
  ISBN-13: 978-1-57886-937-4 (cloth : alk. paper)
  ISBN-10: 1-57886-937-4 (cloth : alk. paper)
  ISBN-13: 978-1-57886-938-1 (pbk. : alk. paper)
  ISBN-10: 1-57886-938-2 (pbk. : alk. paper)
  ISBN-13: 978-1-57886-939-8 (electronic)
  ISBN-10: 1-57886-939-0 (electronic)
  1. Student teachers—Supervision of. I. Lyman, Lawrence. II. Foyle,
Harvey Charles. III. Title.
  LB2157.A3M67 2009
  370.71—dc22   2008034064

370.71
.M67
2009

∞™ The paper used in this publication meets the minimum requirements of
American National Standard for Information Sciences—Permanence of
Paper for Printed Library Materials, ANSI/NISO Z39.48-1992.
Manufactured in the United States of America.

Contents

Foreword

Michael A. Morehead, Lawrence Lyman, and Harvey C. Foyle have been leading authorities on successful practices for working with student teachers for well over two decades. Each of these authors has devoted his career to education and to educating individuals who wish to enter the teaching profession. They understand the complex role of teacher preparation through their professional experiences as P–12 schoolteachers and administrators and as faculty members and administrators in university teacher preparation. *Working with Student Teachers* is a definitive guide for cooperating teachers and university faculty who help mold preservice teachers into well-prepared P–12 classroom teachers. The authors provide specific strategies for effective and supportive supervision, working with challenging student teachers, insuring success in classrooms with a diverse student population, and ongoing communication between the cooperating teacher or university supervisor and the preservice teacher. Literally hundreds of individuals throughout the United States and internationally have participated in workshops focusing on Working with Student Teachers. These participants praise the clarity and relevance of the topics addressed in this book. I know you will find the topics to be a positive resource if you are working with student teachers!

Tes Mehring,
provost/vice president for academic affairs,
Emporia State University in Kansas

Acknowledgments

Special thanks to Nicole A. Hughes, who assisted in editing the second edition. Ms. Hughes has a bachelor's degree from New Mexico State University in English and is employed by the College of Education.

Special thanks to Candace J. Sitzer, who assisted in editing, researching, and guiding the development of the first edition. Ms. Sitzer has a master's degree from New Mexico State University and was employed by the College of Education.

Special thanks also to Tatiana Pachkova, research assistant in the graduate school at Emporia State University, 2000–2001.

Introduction

Student teaching is the capstone of a preservice teacher's professional preparation program. Although university policies and curriculum largely structure the experiences of the preservice teacher prior to the student teaching experience, the final internship has the most influence on a preservice teacher's development. Cooperating teachers and university faculty members assigned to supervise an intern, therefore, play a crucial role in a student teacher's professional growth; they need specific strategies they can use when supervising the instruction and activities of an intern.

Depending upon the type of teaching program that a student enters, a student teacher may be called just that or an intern, intern teacher, or preservice teacher. The classroom teacher may be called a cooperating teacher, a mentor teacher, or a supervising teacher. The teaching program may be called a student teacher program, a professional development school, or an internship program. Even though the programs vary and the designations vary in line with the programs, they all are moving young people from the role of student to teacher. In order to enhance the readability of the text, the authors have decided to use these terms interchangeably. Student teachers will sometimes be referred to as interns or preservice teachers, cooperating teachers as mentors, and university supervisors as supervisors. Also, when referring to the supervision team of the university supervisor, the cooperating teacher, and the principal, the term supervisors may be used.

This book is intended to help cooperating teachers and university supervisors better assist interns during their final stages of preparation.

Necessary skills for these mentors include recognizing and reinforcing appropriate instructional behaviors, helping student teachers clarify decision-making processes, and helping identify solutions to instructional problems. Of particular concern to most supervisors is the student teacher who displays incompetence in the classroom. Strategies for conferencing with interns are outlined in this book, with specific attention given to both incompetent and excellent student teachers.

Each chapter in this book discusses a variety of strategies that can enhance the student teaching experience for both the cooperating teacher and the intern. Chapter 1, "Creating and Sustaining Productive Partnerships," indicates that effective clinical experiences among the various stakeholders are formed in productive partnerships. "Building Positive Relationships" (chapter 2) offers suggestions on how to enhance relations and build trust throughout the experience. Trust is a key element in the relationship between a supervisor and student teacher and is a fragile element that can be easily shaken during the experience. It is most often threatened the first time a mentor has to deal with a behavior exhibited by an intern that needs modification. Suggestions are offered on how to limit the loss of trust when dealing with difficult issues.

Chapter 3, "Student Teaching Program Assessment and Accountability," points out that many assessments are taken of the student intern to determine successful knowledge, skills, and practice. The collected data should be used to systematically improve the program's quality. "Planning and Sequencing" (chapter 4) offers specific examples of introducing the intern into the classroom setting and beginning the teaching experience. Supervision strategies outlined in chapter 5, "Supervising the Student Teacher," suggest specific examples of formative and summative conferences. Also discussed are strategies that can diffuse problems before they begin to threaten the success of the experience for both mentor and intern.

"Helping Student Teachers Succeed in Diverse Classrooms" (chapter 6) discusses teaching strategies and topics that can assist supervisors and student teachers to more effectively work with a diverse population of individuals. It is apparent that diverse populations profoundly influence classrooms today. All teacher education programs today emphasize diversity in their curriculum, so interns should be well grounded academically about pluralistic issues. It is essential that cooperating teachers and university supervisors model appropriate, effective, and educational practice related to diversity.

Chapter 7, "The Incompetent Student Teacher," offers suggestions on when and how to effectively work through difficult situations. Because of the significance of not assigning an intern a passing grade, it is essential that all due process procedures be followed. This chapter helps outline those strategies and offers other suggestions to assist the mentor. Working with an "excellent" student teacher can be just as challenging but in a much different way. Supervisors often erroneously believe that these interns, because of their high performance, need less guidance and assistance. Chapter 8, "The Excellent Student Teacher," outlines several scenarios that a mentor might encounter, from the passive intern who has excellent potential and skills but is not utilizing those skills to the fullest to an overly aggressive one. Excellent interns need as much or more feedback during the student teaching experience as other interns, but they often do not receive extensive supervision.

"The Principal's Role" (chapter 9) outlines examples of activities that the school's educational leader should participate in. The authors realize the complexity of this position and how challenging it is to find time for interns, but as the instructional leader, the principal models the attitudes and sets the tone for others. If a principal takes time for interns, and emphasizes the importance of the interns to others in the building, the entire demeanor of the educational community will be one of acceptance and support.

The preservice teacher needs specific information from the mentor throughout the student teaching experience and especially during the first week. These early conversations ensure a positive start and better communication for the future. University supervisors should verify that the information they provide remains consistent with the university's policies and guidelines for student teaching. Here is a list of helpful materials to share early in the experience:

Seating chart and class roster
School handbook
Copies of or access to teacher's textbook editions
Copies of or access to curriculum guides

Copy of or access to the School Improvement Plan
Daily schedule
Lesson plan book
District and school calendar
Staff roster
School map

THE NEED FOR CONFERENCING SKILLS

Giebelhaus and Bowman indicate that feedback is essential for the professional growth of student teachers.[1] When cooperating teachers are formally trained in assessment, certain areas of an intern's professional growth can be enhanced. Their research indicates that formative feedback in conjunction with formal training of the teacher supervisor has a positive influence on the professional development of the preservice teacher. Conferencing strategies can assist the supervisor in managing and developing the student teacher during the formative phases of the experience.

Caruso indicates that sometimes it is necessary to make difficult decisions related to an intern's professional status.[2] When this is necessary, it is a challenge to all parties. Although school principals can work effectively with student teachers and supervisors within their school setting, the student teaching triad (student teacher, cooperating teacher, and university supervisor) is the foundation of the experience. Interpersonal relationships among these three levels of teachers emerge and are formalized during the conferencing process and are impacted by a variety of local, state, and national demographics. One of these is the changing diverse population within the United States.

The 2000 census shows that the United States changed significantly between 1990 and 2000. In 1990, the population was approximately 249 million, and by 2000, it had grown to 281.4 million, an increase of 13.2 percent. Table I.1 shows the breakdown by race/ethnicity. Also, by 2000, the Hispanic population of 33.1 million almost equaled the black population of 34.7 million.[3]

The ethnicity of those in the teaching profession should mirror that of the general population; however, information available in 1990 indi-

Table I.1.   U.S. Population by Race/Ethnicity, 1990 and 2000 (in percentage)

Ethnicity	1990 Census	2000 Census
White	83.9	75.1
Black	12.3	12.3
Asian	3.0	3.6
Native American	0.8	0.9
Other	—	8.1*

Note: *other races and the new multirace category

cated that this was not the case. The Association of Teacher Educators (ATE) reported, "Prospective teachers are mainly white females from small towns or suburban communities who matriculate in colleges less than 100 miles from home and who intend to return to similar settings to teach."[4] These prospective teachers were 81 percent female and 92 percent white.

The U.S. Department of Education indicates the number of teachers in the United States is increasing. "Between 2004, the last year of actual data, and 2016, the number of teachers in elementary and secondary schools is projected to rise."[5] This increase in numbers applies to both public and private school teachers. The U.S. Department of Education surveys in 1993–1994 and 1999–2000 indicated the racial and ethnic makeup of the teacher population is changing as well.[6]

The enrollment of minority groups in United States schools is increasing.[7] At the same time, the number of minority preservice teachers is increasing.[8] However, these two populations are not equal. For example, the population of black students in schools (1996, 16.9 percent) was not equally matched by the same percentage of preservice teachers going into the profession (1995, 9.0 percent).

The preservice teacher percentages are growing for minority groups but not at the same rate as the general student population. In reference to professional development schools (PDS) and the attempts to solve some of these imbalances, Abdal-Haqq indicates that the professional development schools may actually sustain the imbalance due to stringent entry requirements.

The prevailing imbalance in the teaching force, that is, the percentage of racial, ethnic, and linguistic minority students is increasing while the percentage of teachers from these groups is decreasing or not keeping pace. . . . Although cultural congruence is not a guarantee of effective teaching, diversity literature does confirm that it has important advantages for minority group students. In addition, a diverse teaching force benefits all children and professional educators because it exposes them to different perspectives and provides them with opportunities to expand their views about who has the power that comes from knowledge and skill.[9]

What does all of this information about demographics have to do with various approaches to conferences with student teachers? Conferencing skills based in research and practice are appropriate across racial/ethnic boundaries. There are two factors to consider. All teachers will need training in conferencing skills in order to be an effective cooperating teacher and conduct effective conferences with parents, students, or other educators. Also, as the number of minority students increases, current nonminority teachers will need to be educated about strategies for conferencing with minority preservice teachers, visiting with parents from differing racial or ethnic backgrounds, and interacting with administrators who are from different populations. A significant population change is occurring in the United States and in the schools. Conferences are important and should become a part of all teachers' and administrators' repertoire of skills. For student teachers and beginning teachers, induction programs, such as professional development schools and teacher professional year-long induction workshops and mentoring programs, provide a focus to support and retain teachers.[10] All of the persons involved in teacher education at all levels must be the best and do their best when working with students. This is why the title of this book is *Working with Student Teachers: Getting and Giving the Best*.

NOTES

1. Carman Giebelhaus and Connie Bowman, "Teaching Mentors: Is It Worth the Effort?" (paper presented at the annual meeting of the Association of Teacher Educators, Orlando, Fla., February 2000), 1–24.

2. Joseph J. Caruso, "Cooperating Teacher and Student Teacher Phases of Development," *Young Children* 55, no. 1 (January 2000): 75–81.

3. Lewis Mumford Center, University of Albany, "A Nation Ablaze with Change," *USA Today*, July 3, 2001, 4(A).

4. Association of Teacher Educators, "Improve Recruitment and Selection," in *Restructuring the Education of Teachers: Report of the Commission on the Education of Teachers into the 21st Century* (Reston, Va.: Association of Teacher Educators, 1991), 16.

5. National Center for Education Statistics, "Projections of Education Statistics to 2016, Section 5. Elementary and Secondary Teachers: Introduction." Retrieved February 3, 2008, from nces.ed.gov/programs/projections/projections 2016/sec5a.asp.

6. American Association of Colleges for Teacher Education (AACTE), "Public Elementary and Secondary School Teachers, by Race/Ethnicity, 1993–1994 and 1999–2000 (in Percent)." U.S. Department of Education, National Center for Education Statistics Mini-Digest of Education Statistics, 2003. Retrieved February 3, 2008, from www.aacte.org/programs/multicultural/ enrollment_ethnicity_yr93-94.aspx.

7. National Center for Education Statistics. "Minority Enrollment: Percentage Distribution of the Race/Ethnicity of Public School Students in Kindergarten through 12th Grade, by Region: Fall 1972 and 2005." U.S. Department of Commerce, Census Bureau, Current Population Survey (CPS), October Supplement, 1972 and 2005. Retrieved February 3, 2008, from nces.ed.gov/programs/coe/2007/charts/chart05.asp.

8. American Association of Colleges for Teacher Education (AACTE), "SCDE Enrollments by Race and Ethnicity, 1989, 1991, 1995 and 2001." AACTE, *Survey of Teacher Education Enrollments by Race/Ethnicity and Gender, Fall 1989, 1991, and 1995*. PEDS 2002. Retrieved February 3, 2008, from www.aacte.org/programs/multicultural/enrollment_ethnicity_yr89-91-95 .aspx.

9. Ismat Abdal-Haqq, *Voices of Caution: Equity Issues, Professional Development Schools: Weighing the Evidence* (Thousand Oaks, Calif.: Corwin Press, 1999), 66–67.

10. National Education Association, "Attracting and Keeping Quality Teachers." Retrieved February 3, 2008, from www.nea.org/teachershortage/ index.html. Also in Phi Delta Kappa, *Teacher to Teacher*. Retrieved February 3, 2008, from www.pdkintl.org/t2t/t2thome.htm.

CHAPTER 1

Creating and Sustaining Productive Partnerships

ADVANTAGES OF PRODUCTIVE PARTNERSHIPS

Partnerships between educators representing various agencies and constituencies involved in the preparation of new teachers can have many advantages. Increasing the amount of time spent in clinical settings, such as professional development schools, provides hands-on experiences that help future teachers practice and refine their teaching skills. Additional input into program design, curriculum, and assessment from sources outside the university helps to increase the relevance of teacher education preparation and prepare future teachers for the "real world" of teaching.

Partnerships can improve the quantity and quality of feedback given to the future teacher and help to assure that the clinical experiences of future teachers are as productive and positive as possible. Partnerships can provide opportunities for colleagues to evaluate the effectiveness of teacher education initiatives and make needed changes and improvements. Opportunities to work together as partners can make effective use of limited resources and improve the quality of teacher preparation.

As universities and school districts work together to create professional development school partnerships, P–12 students benefit from having extra assistance from future teachers in the classroom. Schools and districts also benefit from the opportunity to evaluate potential candidates for teaching positions as they are working in the professional development school and recruit the candidates best suited for the school and district.

CHARACTERISTICS OF PRODUCTIVE PARTNERSHIPS

Sense of mission. Educators in productive partnerships have a sense that collaborating together is necessary to address urgent needs. In the case of teacher education, partnerships can work together to address issues that may include:

- preparation of teachers to meet the needs of increasingly diverse students;
- recruitment of new teachers to meet the needs of growing school populations and retiring teachers;
- recruitment of minority teachers;
- recruitment of teachers for high needs areas;
- reducing attrition of beginning teachers in the first three to five years of teaching;
- addressing public concerns about the quality of P–12 education and about teacher preparation;
- and reducing the cost of completing a teacher education program for future teachers.

Shared goals and vision. An important part of a productive partnership is the articulation of the common goals and beliefs shared by the educators in the partnership. The development of specific goals, accompanied by desired outcomes and assessment strategies, is the first task of any productive partnership effort. Agreement on the roles and responsibilities of those involved is necessary to insure the success of the partnerships.

Time. In partnerships which are productive, there is a willingness to spend the time necessary to analyze teacher education standards and desired subject matter outcomes to determine how these standards and outcomes can be most productively achieved. Creating a cohesive, aligned teacher education curriculum which maximizes the time the future teacher spends in a clinical setting working with students requires careful planning and flexibility.

Time is also required to evaluate the effectiveness of the partnership. Such evaluation requires the analysis of data, discussion of positive and negative results, and planning for improvement.

Mutual respect. Productive partnerships between educational agencies are characterized by mutual respect between the educators involved. Each of the constituencies involved in the partnership must respect the professionalism and expertise of the others. Because partnership efforts often involve changes which can seem uncomfortable or threatening to some participants, respect for the comfort levels, personalities, and professional concerns of colleagues is essential. Disagreements, which will inevitably occur when working together, must be resolved in positive, creative ways that respect the dignity of all involved.

Restructuring. In partnerships that are productive, resources are creatively and appropriately shared. Facilities, supplies, and personnel are among the resources that can be analyzed to determine the most efficient and effective way to meet the needs of future teachers.

Administrative support. The support of the administrators of the educators involved in partnerships is essential. Productive partnerships are sanctioned, encouraged, and supported with appropriate resources. Collaborative partnerships are encouraged and rewarded.

Celebration. Successful collaboration requires celebration of successes achieved as a result of partnership efforts. It is especially important, given the amount of negative publicity about schools and colleges of teacher education, that successful efforts to enhance the quality of teacher preparation and the success of P–12 students be celebrated and disseminated.

PROFESSIONAL DEVELOPMENT SCHOOL PARTNERSHIPS

Professional development schools have emerged as one of the most promising partnerships between university and P–12 educators (see table 1.1). Traditional student teaching programs should consider the advantages of this model for their own students.

Professional development schools offer future teachers the opportunity to interact with students in a clinical setting with extended time for future teachers to practice and refine their planning, teaching, and assessment skills in a clinical setting that has been compared to a "teaching hospital."[1] One of the most important advantages for the future

Table 1.1.   Desired Outcomes of Professional Development School Partnerships

1. The professional development school improves the preparation of future teachers.
2. The professional development school offers professional development opportunities for P–12 teachers.
3. The professional development school offers professional development opportunities for university faculty.
4. The professional development school positively affects the achievement of P–12 students.

teacher is the increased opportunities for feedback from the trained mentor teacher in addition to the university supervisor.

Because future teachers are often involved in methods classes while participating in the professional development school, another advantage is the opportunity to apply learning from methods classes in a "real life" setting. Future teachers are able to focus planning, teaching, and assessment on actual students and classroom situations that occur as part of their clinical experiences.

Professional development school partnerships offer professional development opportunities for P–12 cooperating teachers who work with future teachers. To be successful, cooperating teachers need to receive training in effective communication, supervision strategies, and assessment of student teachers as outlined in the subsequent chapters of this book.

Cooperating teacher training can enhance the professional skills of the cooperating teacher. As the cooperating teacher articulates reasons for teaching decisions he or she is making, the cooperating teacher engages in critical thinking about his or her teaching practice. As they observe student teachers using innovative teaching strategies, some cooperating teachers are encouraged to learn about these strategies and apply the strategies in the classroom setting.

For P–12 cooperating teachers, the opportunity to interact with eager and enthusiastic student teachers is often exhilarating and can help to reduce stress and burnout. Opportunities to present at professional conferences, to participate in grant writing with university faculty, and to demonstrate effective teaching strategies for future teachers can also enhance the satisfaction and competence of the cooperating teacher.

University faculty can also benefit from productive professional development school partnerships. As faculty members interact with cooperating teachers and their students, they get an important "reality check" about the increasing diversity and complexity of the P–12 classroom. When sufficient trust is built with cooperating teachers and administrators, university faculty can use P–12 classrooms to demonstrate strategies for their student teachers, to conduct research, and to enhance their professional skills.

Participation in a professional development school partnership can encourage university faculty to return to P–12 classrooms for extended periods of time.[2] When university faculty work in P–12 classrooms, there is more help available for the students in those classrooms and faculty can stay up to date on the issues impacting teachers, students, and schools. Future teachers can benefit from interacting with their professors in actual classroom settings as well.

As with the P–12 teacher, professional development school experiences can provide opportunities for professional presentations and publications, for grant writing, and for improving professional skills. These opportunities can help the faculty member meet university requirements for tenure, promotion, and service.

P–12 teachers and administrators and university faculty report improvements in student achievement and attitude when future teachers interact with students as part of the professional development school. Other benefits may include future teachers becoming more creative and ambitious in planning lessons and opportunities for action research in the classroom.[3]

CURRICULUM IN A PROFESSIONAL DEVELOPMENT SCHOOL

There are many advantages to increasing the amount of time a student teacher spends in a professional development school site. A major challenge, however, is to assure that the future teacher acquires the pedagogical knowledge and skills required of beginning teachers. Ideally, methods instructors and cooperating teachers and administrators meet together and determine which experiences and practice opportunities can be found at the professional development school site.

One of the challenges in restructuring the methods curriculum is that "we are rebuilding the airplane while it's in flight."[4] Educators at all levels are overworked and overscheduled. Finding time for any new endeavor is often difficult. It requires a significant commitment of time to analyze the state standards and subject matter expectations traditionally taught in methods classes and to come up with creative ways to meet these standards and expectations in the "real world" setting of the professional development school.

Another challenge is the unwillingness of some university instructors to "let go" of some of the content of their classes. Relationships need to be built between university instructors and public school teachers so that the instructors are confident that some of the standards and expectations can be efficiently and appropriately met in the professional development school setting.

In analyzing the challenges of faculty-led improvement activities, Robert McClure notes that "if it's not local, it's not real."[5] For restructuring the delivery of the teacher education curriculum, this means that future teachers will find different curriculum models, teaching strategies, and management styles in different professional development school classrooms and schools. It is necessary, therefore, to track each of the standards and expected outcomes and to be open to different ways in which these standards and outcomes may be met in different districts and schools.

An example may be helpful at this point. Consider the elementary reading methods instructor. This instructor has demonstrated a variety of reading strategies such as guided reading, reader's theater, use of "big books" for younger students, and literature circles for upper elementary students. Traditionally, the instructor has used simulations, taped instructional sequences, and small group teaching to demonstrate these strategies in the university classroom.

Through discussion with public school colleagues and observation in their classrooms, the instructor determines that these strategies are used appropriately by cooperating teachers at various grade levels in the school. By planning together, the instructor and cooperating teachers agree that the future teachers will observe each of these strategies in the professional development school setting by observing in various classrooms when the strategies are demonstrated and writing an analysis of how the strategy was demonstrated by the teacher.

This plan requires that the primary teacher who is utilizing a big book as part of a reading lesson lets the future teachers at the professional development school site know when she is planning to teach the lesson. The future teachers come to observe the lesson and complete the required assignment for the university instructor. The upper grade teacher also lets the future teachers know when his students are working in literature circles. When interns come to observe, each intern observes one small group in the class. The future teachers meet together after the observation and discuss how the circle they observed functioned.

Restructuring the teacher education curriculum obviously requires a great deal of planning and flexibility. Cooperating teachers may be hesitant to allow several future teachers to observe in the classroom at one time. It is important to clearly set the guidelines for such observations. The future teachers are not rating or evaluating the teaching of the cooperating teacher—they are analyzing how a specific strategy they learned about in the university classroom is applied in a "real" setting.

In some settings, the cooperating teacher may be comfortable with the university instructor demonstrating a specific strategy in their classroom while the future teachers observe.

Table 1.2.   Cooperating Teacher Rating
for Classroom Management Observations

Cooperative Teacher Rating of the Intern's Observation Guide

Rating scale for each item:

1	2	3	4	5
strongly disagree	disagree	neutral	agree	strongly agree

1. All required information from the observation guide is completed.	1	2	3	4	5
2. No personally identifiable information about students is included.	1	2	3	4	5
3. Teaching strategies identified are accurate.	1	2	3	4	5
4. Intern can describe rules of the classroom and consequences accurately.	1	2	3	4	5
5. Intern can describe emergency procedures for the classroom accurately.	1	2	3	4	5

This allows the university instructor to model the implementation of a strategy that a cooperating teacher may be uncertain about. As the future teachers observe their university instructor teaching, they may be joined by other classroom teachers at the professional development school site who want to observe the strategy. The classroom teachers who observe may want additional instruction and coaching which the university instructor can provide.

Another example of restructuring the curriculum can be found in classroom management class. The classroom management instructor wants future teachers to observe their assigned students using the Classroom Observation Guide (table 4.3, chapter 4). After observing and making notes, the future teacher meets with the cooperating teacher who rates the accuracy of the observations. A rubric, developed by the university instructor with input from the cooperating teachers, is used by the cooperating teacher for the rating which is turned in to the university instructor.

There are several advantages for having the cooperating teacher participate in the rating of this assignment. The cooperating teacher obviously knows and understands the students in his or her classroom and is in a much better position to rate the accuracy of the future teacher's observations of the students and of the cooperating teacher's strategies for working with the students. The future teacher is required to apply his or her knowledge of students in the classroom where he or she will be working. If a particular observation is inaccurate, the university instructor can provide remedial activities as needed.

The most valuable activities for future teachers involve working with individual students, small groups, and the whole class in the professional development school setting. Planning assignments with the cooperating teachers and making sure that future teachers have opportunities to apply what they are learning by planning, implementing, and assessing instruction in a "real" classroom help to provide needed practice for future teachers as they are actually involved in learning the methods content.

PARTNERSHIPS WITH COMMUNITY COLLEGES

Many teacher education students complete all or part of their general education requirements at a community college. Partnerships between universities and community colleges can provide opportunities to make transfers from community colleges to university teacher education programs more efficient. Publications and web sites can provide assistance in long-term planning. Meetings between community college advisors and university advisors can help each better meet the needs of the teacher education student.[6] With teacher shortages projected and the cost of teacher education tuition, fees, and supplies rising, attracting more teachers into the profession is an important goal. Minority teachers are especially needed.[7] When universities partner with community colleges located in urban areas to share the delivery of the teacher education curriculum on the community college campus site, nontraditional students and future teachers who are place-bound because of family or job needs can complete requirements for teacher education closer to their homes. Future teachers complete the community college courses aligned with the university teacher education program. The students can continue at the community college site with teacher education courses offered by university faculty.

When universities work together with community colleges, tutorial services for students can be utilized at both sites to assist teacher education students in meeting program requirements. Financial aid and admission procedures can be coordinated so that the student moves from the community college program to the university teacher education program smoothly.[8]

PARTNERSHIPS FOR RECRUITING NEW TEACHER CANDIDATES

Because of the need to recruit teachers to replace teachers leaving the profession, to meet shortages in subject matter areas such as math, science, and technology, and to meet the needs of an increasingly diverse P–12 student population, recruiting qualified candidates into teacher education programs is an important challenge. One strategy for recruiting new teachers is to provide high school students with an opportunity to learn about the teaching profession and think about themselves as potential future teachers.

An example is the Kansas Future Teacher Academy, funded by the Kansas legislature. Since the inception of the academy in 1989, over 800 high school students have participated in the academy. The academy meets for five days during the summer on the campus of Emporia State University. Through interaction with guest speakers, including National Teacher Hall of Fame inductees, National State Teachers of the Year, Kansas master teachers, and university faculty, academy participants explore the profession of teaching, match interests and abilities they have to the requirements of teaching, and set goals for the remainder of their high school experience.[9]

Admission to the Kansas Future Teacher Academy is open to public and private high school students. Contacts with high school administrators and counselors help to spread the word about the academy and attract potential attendees. Graduates of the academy are encouraged to recruit younger students at their high schools to attend the academy in future years.

Since attracting minority candidates to teaching is a continuing challenge, another future teacher academy strategy targets middle school students identified by their teachers and counselors to be good candidates for teaching. School districts and universities can work together to bring the identified middle school students to a university campus for a day where the students can interact with each other, with faculty from the school districts, and with university faculty.

SUSTAINING PRODUCTIVE PARTNERSHIPS

Successful partnerships require nurturing in order to sustain the successful outcomes of collaboration. Strategies for sustaining productive partnerships include:

- *Keep in touch*. Continue to schedule regular meetings of the partnership members to discuss problems, make changes, look for ways to enhance the partnership, and celebrate successes.
- *New membership*. Encourage new staff members to become involved in partnership efforts. New members can help to build on the energy and enthusiasm of the partnership.
- *Dissemination opportunities*. Look for ways to expand the effectiveness of the partnership through grants, professional publication, and conference presentations.

- *Rituals and ceremonies.* Creating rituals and ceremonies can enhance the partnership. For example, an open house ceremony can welcome new partners and provide an opportunity for participants from various agencies to get together at the start of a new school year.
- *Involve graduates.* Teacher education program graduates who become successful teachers are some of the best public relations representatives for partnership efforts. Graduates can be guest speakers for new groups of teacher education students, offering ideas for success and encouragement from those who have "made it." As conference presenters and collaborators on articles, graduates can share personal experiences and insights about the effectiveness of partnership efforts.

CHAPTER SUMMARY

The challenges facing P–12 schools, community colleges, and universities involved in the preparation of future teachers mandate the need for effective partnerships to make creative and cost-effective use of available resources. Creating effective partnerships requires a commitment of time, energy, and resources for collaboration. Mutual respect and trust must be developed between the stakeholders to assure that the best possible teacher education experience is provided for the future teacher. Increasing the amount of time spent in clinical settings reaffirms the need to train P–12 teachers and administrators in effective supervision practices to maximize the effectiveness of the clinical experience for the future teacher, mentor, university faculty, and the P–12 student.

NOTES

1. Arthur Levine, *Educating School Teachers* (Washington, D.C.: The Education Schools Project, 2006), 9.

2. Lawrence Lyman, "A Professor Returns to the Classroom in a Professional Development School," ERIC Resources in Education (paper presented at the national conference of the Kansas University Professional Development Schools Alliance, Kansas City, Mo., February 2000).

3. Michelle Hammond, "Professional Development Schools: Synergy at Its Finest," *School-University Partnerships* 1, no. 2 (Fall 2007): 6–8.

4. Robert M. McClure, "School Improvement through Colleagueship and Cooperation," in *Cooperative Grouping for Interactive Learning: Students, Teachers, and Administrators*, edited by Lawrence Lyman and Harvey C. Foyle (Washington, D.C.: National Education Association, 1990), 8.

5. McClure, "School Improvement through Colleagueship and Cooperation," 8.

6. Lori A. Mann and Lawrence Lyman, "Enhancing Public School and University Professional Development School Partnerships: The Community College Link," *School-University Partnerships* 1, no. 1 (Spring 2007): 81.

7. Cynthia Kopkowski, "My Debt, My Life," *NEA Today*, no. 26 (January, 4, 2008): 29–33.

8. Mann and Lyman, "Enhancing Public School and University Professional Development School Partnerships," 80–82.

9. Jones Institute for Educational Excellence, "Kansas Future Teacher Academy." Retrieved January 8, 2008, from www.emporia.edu/jones/kfta/index/htm.

CHAPTER 2

Building Positive Relationships

The cooperating teacher provides critical support and guidance for the intern assigned to her class. The mentor helps ensure a positive student teaching experience by developing an affirmative professional relationship, supervising the intern's work competency, and evaluating progress. Table 2.1 represents the skills needed by the cooperating teacher in order to assist an intern's growth professional and provide a supportive atmosphere.

It is important to remember that the mentor provides opportunities for the student teacher success during the practicum experience. Even the most caring and competent teacher cannot guarantee the success of an intern in a specific classroom setting. Skills that the student teacher brings to the practicum, however, often determine the degree of success he will experience. The attitude, maturity, and work ethic will also affect the quality of the student teacher's experience. These factors are usually beyond the control of the mentor teacher.

Table 2.1. Mentor Teacher Skills

Modeling and Explaining	Planning Skills	Supervision Skills
Good teaching practices	Instructional planning	Collecting data
Positive, professional attitude	Sequencing the student	Reinforcing
Communication skills	Teaching experience	Brainstorming
Remediating		
Building trust		
Positive regard		

INITIAL CONTACT WITH THE PROSPECTIVE STUDENT TEACHER

Interviewing

A positive relationship often begins when the cooperating teacher interviews the prospective student teacher prior to beginning the teaching experience. An interview of twenty to thirty minutes lets a mentor become acquainted with the student teacher and may identify potential problems or conflicts that need to be addressed before a placement is finalized. Interviews can assist both parties in determining if the setting is appropriate. A list of possible interview questions is provided in table 2.2.

When meeting for the first time, the mentor needs to realize that an intern will be nervous and might appear to lack confidence.[1] It is important to remember that the student teacher is at an early stage in professional development and will usually gain confidence while becoming familiar with the mentor and students.

A potential problem for some teachers is the comparison of the prospective intern with another whom the mentor supervised previously. Such comparisons are almost always unfair to both the previous student teacher and the prospective intern. Mentors need to be aware of

Table 2.2.   Interview Questions for Prospective Student Teachers

These questions were adapted from a list created by professional development school coordinators from Emporia State University and mentor teachers and principals from professional development schools in the Emporia (Kansas) and Olathe (Kansas) Public Schools. Mentor teachers should select questions from the list that will elicit the information most important to them.

1. Tell me about yourself.
2. Why do you want to be a teacher?
3. Why are you interested in student teaching at this grade level? Why are you interested in student teaching at this school?
4. What kinds of experiences have you had with children? Have you had experiences with culturally diverse groups of students?
5. Tell me about a student with whom you have worked and who was a real challenge for you.
6. What is your philosophy of teaching?
7. As a student, what subjects do you like best and why?
8. What are your strengths?
9. Tell me about a teacher who had a strong positive influence on you.

the human tendency to make such comparisons and be careful to judge each prospective student teacher on her own merits.

Developing a Positive Relationship

The professional relationship between the intern and the mentor is crucial to the student teacher's success.[2] A positive, professional relationship can help make the student teacher feel comfortable in the classroom. Additionally, when interns feel accepted, they are more likely to demonstrate positive attitudes toward students and adults in the school, and give a genuine effort in the assignment. A positive, professional relationship requires that the mentor be a competent professional who models good teaching practices and is capable of articulating his reasons for teaching decisions. A mentor's positive, professional attitude toward teaching, students, colleagues, and parents is a crucial model for the student teacher's development of attitudes and behaviors. The cooperating teacher must communicate positively and effectively so that necessary information about the teaching context is communicated. Building trust with the student teacher will evolve from this open and positive communication approach.

The cooperating teacher as the instructional leader must be responsible for providing feedback and guidance to the preservice teacher. As Kouzes and Posner point out, "Strategies, tactics, skills, and practices are empty unless we understand the fundamental human aspirations that connect leaders and their consitutents."[3]

PREREQUISITE MENTOR TEACHER SKILLS AND ATTITUDES

To be effective, a mentor must first be a competent teacher in the classroom and must model behaviors and attitudes expected of good teachers. One of the most critical areas of a mentor's performance in the classroom is the ability to establish and maintain a positive learning environment for all students. If this component of effective teaching is lacking, the student teacher will almost certainly be better served in another classroom. The placement of an intern is not to support or assist a mediocre or poor teacher. As cooperating teacher placements are considered, it is essential that the most dedicated and best teachers be given first priority.

Not all educators who are effective teachers of K–12 students are equally as effective working with student teachers. Identifying and articulating teaching decisions are important skills for cooperating teachers. This requires a mentor to be confident in making teaching decisions and not be threatened or uneasy when questioned about these decisions by a preservice student. Thinking about the reasons why a teaching decision was made and articulating those reasons is a metacognitive process that provides professional growth for the mentor a well as the intern.[4]

A cooperating teacher must be willing to accept input from the intern about observations of the teaching and learning processes occurring in the classroom. One of the most rewarding aspects of a student teacher is having another set of eyes viewing the students in the classroom. Like all good teachers, mentors must make use of all available input and ideas to improve their interactions with students. Because teachers are required to make so many decisions each day, some decisions could be clarified and improved upon thorough reflection and discussion with an intern.[5]

Finally, cooperating teachers must be willing to share their classrooms and students with another professional. Some capable classroom teachers are simply not comfortable in relinquishing control of their students to another. If so, the intern and the students in the classroom may sense their reluctance. If the mentor's reluctance is obvious, the intern's experience is less likely to be successful.

Insisting that the intern use only strategies and methods of teaching used by the mentor is another indication of unwillingness to relinquish control. Problems in sharing the classroom and students are sometimes evidenced if the mentor teacher feels the need to publicly correct the intern while he is teaching. Although public suggestions may be necessary at time, such corrections will undermine the credibility of the student teacher. If an intern is corrected publicly numerous times, students will stop listening to the intern and begin turning to the teacher, causing the intern to lose trust in the mentor.

If it becomes necessary for the mentor to intervene, using a phrase like "Have you thought of describing it this way?" will be a more effective approach to the situation. The mentor may also want to develop a signal that indicates to the student teacher there is a need to discuss something immediately. As the semester progresses, more freedom must be granted to the intern. Allowing the student teacher to try different strategies and methods usually benefits both the intern and the students in the classroom.

Positive, Professional Attitude

Mentors must demonstrate a positive and professional attitude toward teaching, students, parents, and colleagues when working with an intern. A myriad of challenges face every classroom teacher, but cynicism and negative approaches are discouraging and draining for all professionals. A cooperating teacher with a negative attitude can be debilitating to even the most enthusiastic beginning teacher. Mentors who view teaching as an exciting and rewarding profession are the best models for future teachers. These mentors are characterized by their willingness to try new ideas and methods with all students. Their classrooms are exciting, vibrant places where children are actively and positively engaged in appropriate learning experiences.

Good mentors demonstrate positive relationships with students, and classroom management is accomplished while protecting the dignity of the students. Mentors should demonstrate equity in dealing with students and be regarded by students as fair and consistent. A high expectation for the learning and success of all students is a hallmark of a good mentor's classrooms. This standard should be modeled in practice by the mentor, expected of the students, and required of the intern. These three elements will improve the likelihood of the intern's success.

The mentor must consistently model professionalism while dealing with colleagues, administrators, and parents. The cooperating teacher must resist the urge to share negative feelings and attitudes toward another teacher, principal, student, or parent. This may be difficult in schools where gossip in the faculty lounge is the norm, but the mentor must set the tone for professional behavior and overcome other negative models observed by a student teacher. Sharing confidential information about colleagues, parents, or administrators must be done only in the context of a "need to know" basis. If, in the judgment of the cooperating teacher, an intern needs to know something to assist him in performing his task better, the mentor may need to discuss this information.

Communication Skills

The ideal student teaching experience is characterized by many opportunities to share ideas and information, both formally and informally. Effective communication requires the mentor to demonstrate skills of listening, sharing information, and giving feedback.

Listening effectively to others is a vital communication skill. Covey describes, "If I were to summarize in one sentence the single most important principle I have learned in the field of interpersonal relations, it would be this: Seek first to understand, then to be understood."[6] If the mentor is communicating, she must seek to understand the points of view, the educational decision-making processes, and the concerns of the student teacher.

Effective listening takes time. The cooperating teacher must find time in an already busy and overcrowded schedule to meet with the intern on a regular basis. During these meetings, a mentor should make the effort to communicate and demonstrate all of the characteristics of good listening and communicating effectively. By putting other tasks aside and taking the time to listen, the mentor lets the student teacher know that his ideas are important and encourages sharing ideas. Demonstrating active listening skills while communicating with the intern will improve interpersonal relations and foster an environment of trust. Active listeners use several techniques to accomplish goals, such as making comments, asking questions to draw the speaker out, and attempting to gather further information. They also use body language, including eye contact, posture, and positive facial expressions. Finally, asking questions to clarify the point of view of the student teacher is an important strategy for effective communication.

Positive communication with the student teacher can also be enhanced through the use of affirmation statements. These statements can be used to encourage an intern encountering difficulties with certain aspects of teaching or student relations. Affirmation statements can also be used to remind a student teacher of beliefs or ideals. For example, assure the student teacher that all students can learn and persistence promotes student success. Another use for the affirmation statement is to indicate that the cooperating teacher has faith in the student teacher's ability to solve a problem. For example, the mentor should assure the intern that he has the skills to plan well-organized lessons. The cooperating teacher should let the intern know it will take time at first, but that improvement will be seen quickly. Affirmation statements that reflect the mentor's true attitudes and are delivered without sarcasm or hidden agendas can facilitate positive communication, even in potentially negative situations.

Effective Feedback

One of the most important functions of the cooperating teacher is to provide feedback about instructional performance. Effective feedback has five characteristics: amount, specificity, frequency, timing, and relevancy.

Amount

The amount of feedback given to a student teacher needs to be appropriate. Too much feedback can confuse an intern and be difficult to apply. Too little feedback may inhibit the growth of the student teacher. In formative conferences with an intern, concentrating on one or two specific areas to maintain, change, or improve instruction is advisable. Focusing on only one or two key themes will give the mentor an opportunity to determine if the student teacher is able to apply the feedback and recommendations.

Specificity

Feedback shared by the cooperating teacher using specific examples from the intern's daily instructional techniques can enhance understanding and performance. Regular, specific feedback can improve an intern's ability to implement recommendations and, therefore, impact the learning of students in a positive manner. Suggestions for action need to focus on improving and modifying instructional strategies.

Specific and clearly defined recommendations benefit the intern by clarifying performance expectations.

Frequency

Frequency refers to how often feedback is provided. Usually, shorter, more frequent conferences are preferable. Short conferences can be informative and put the student teacher at ease. Frequency will likely occur at two key times. One is early in the experience when expectations are being clarified, usually daily, and sometimes hourly. The second time would occur if the intern is having difficulties performing at an acceptable standard. Consequently, frequent conferences and feedback are essential to the success of the relationship.

Timing

Feedback should be timed so it can be useful to the student. In the early weeks of the experience, feedback is usually most effective because the intern has many opportunities to apply the recommendations. Also, mentors should be sensitive to the timing of feedback after a stressful experience. Most interns need reassurance from the cooperating teacher. Specific suggestions for changes as soon as possible after teaching, particularly in the early stages of an assignment, can help a student teacher succeed.

Relevancy

The best feedback will be relevant and specific. Relevant feedback is specific and deals with issues that impart instruction and student learning during the lesson. For example, if two students are off task and the cooperating teacher addresses that behavior through questions or guided discussion, that is relevancy. If the mentor decides to discuss lesson plans and ignores discussing off-task students with the intern because she is fearful it might impact the intern's confidence, that is irrelevant. Useful suggestions from the mentor can help the student teacher gain confidence and make needed improvements. Effective communication is the by-product of the mentor's genuine desire to understand the feelings and attitudes of the student teacher. This is a very important element in the process of building trust with the student teacher.

Building Trust with the Student Teacher

Developing a climate of trust with the student teacher is necessary for effective supervision to take place.[7] According to Lyman et al., teachers in general have legitimate concerns about the process of assessing their competence.[8] When trust between intern and mentor is present, the student teacher will more likely be successful in the assignment.

Two kinds of trust are important: interpersonal and procedural trust. Interpersonal trust is created when the intern feels that difficult issues with the mentor can be discussed without having the information used negatively or communicated inappropriately to a third party. For example, the student teacher may confide to the cooperating teacher that the workload is causing stress. Trust would be diminished considerably if the mentor were to share this information with other practicing teachers in the teachers' lounge.

Interpersonal trust is enhanced when an intern feels that personal feelings and property are treated with respect and dignity. With so much to do, it is easy for a mentor to inadvertently disregard a student teacher's feelings with an unintended remark. When interpersonal trust is present, both parties feel comfortable sharing concerns and resolving problems quickly.

It is also important that the student teacher have a physical space within the classroom that is professional, private, and secure and where professional and personal items can be stored. Both the students in the classroom and the mentor need to respect this personal space. The mentor should establish an environment in the classroom so this can occur.

Procedural trust is built when the intern knows that the cooperating teacher clearly understand the expectations and policies regarding the assignment. An intern has the right to expect the mentor and university supervisor to abide by rules and regulations set forth in university documents and procedure manuals. A common concern occurs when the student teacher is asked to substitute for the mentor when the mentor is absent from the classroom. This request almost always violates the university's policy for student teaching and may violate district policy and state law.[9]

Procedural trust is enhanced when the mentor and university supervisor adhere to schedules indicated by the university. For example, if a weekly conference between the cooperating teacher and intern is indicated by university policy, the mentor should make such a conference a priority, even if time considerations limit the length of such a conference. University supervisors should be careful to make the number of visits to the classroom as directed by the university, meet within the prescribed length of time, and utilize the appropriate forms for giving formative and summative feedback during each visit.

Lyman, Morehead, and Foyle have identified a number of additional factors that build teacher trust. These factors include positive tone, clear expectations, useful feedback, and concern for the student teacher.[10]

Positive tone during interactions with interns results from the mentor focusing on the intern's strengths and positive actions. It is important for student teachers to have a clear understanding of what is done well in the classroom so that these skills can be applied in further student teaching experiences, job interviews, and in their own classrooms.

It is important that the intern know what the teacher expects and that the information needed about the teacher context is provided. Mentors need to make clear standards for effective teaching, as well as any "pet peeves." This may seem insignificant, but many student teaching experiences have turned sour because an intern was unaware of a particular expectation of a cooperating teacher. For example, a particular way to grade, a desire to complete a section of material, or not being punctual can cause a mentor to become irritated with a student teacher. Clarifying these pet peeves or concerns early on will most likely alleviate future problems. Below is a list of desired behaviors that may help the mentor clarify expectations for a student teacher.

List of Behaviors Clarifying Cooperating Teacher Expectations

- Attendance
- Attention to detail

- Attitude toward students
- Attitude toward supervision
- Attitude toward teaching
- Communicating with parents
- Completing tasks on time
- Content knowledge
- Dress of student teacher
- Enthusiasm for teaching
- Evaluating student work
- Following procedures developed by cooperating teacher
- Planning effectively
- Projecting confidence to students
- Punctuality (starting time)
- Quality of written work
- Relations with administration
- Relations with faculty/staff
- Student-centered approach to teaching
- Tactful approval
- Turning in lesson plans (who/where)
- What to do when absent

Concern for the intern can be demonstrated in numerous ways. One of the most important is providing information about the school environment. Specific information about the context of the school and classroom in which the student teacher will be working is needed. Taking time to orient the intern to important personnel, locations of pertinent offices, school procedures, and culture help an intern feel at ease and may avoid problems.

As indicated earlier, useful feedback builds trust. Feedback that recognizes unique strengths and qualities lets the intern know he is valued and appreciated by the mentor. By identifying strengths and discussing them, a mentor will improve relations and trust. Focusing on teaching behaviors rather than on personal traits when giving feedback provides the student teacher with the best opportunity to make positive changes that impact teaching.

Communicating Positive Regard for Student Teachers

Mentors can demonstrate their support for an intern by communicating positive regard. As professionals, student teachers need to feel that their efforts are appreciated and that they are making a positive difference in their assignments. The cooperating teacher can communicate positive regard and build confidence by using the following strategies.

Showing consideration

Goal: For the mentor to demonstrate a caring approach.

- "I know you weren't feeling well yesterday. Are you feeling better today?"
- "How are you doing in your evening class?"
- "I heard you had a great interview. Congratulations."

Showing appreciation

Goal: For the mentor to recognize and value effort.

- "Thanks for all your hard work on that bulletin board. It looks great."
- "I appreciate the way you have been working with Dudley. His attitude is improving."
- "It's such a help to have you here."

Sharing positive feedback

Goal: For the mentor to share positive feedback from others.

- "The substitute yesterday said you did a great job with the class."
- "The principal told me how well you handled the disruption on the playground today."
- "Amy's mother told me how pleased she was with the creative writing lessons you are teaching."

Giving positive feedback about instruction

Goal: For the mentor to share positive observation about instruction.

- "The class scores on that test were very impressive."
- "You handled that student's incorrect answer expertly."
- "Every student had a chance to participate successfully this morning."

CHAPTER SUMMARY

Developing a positive relationship requires effort on the part of both the mentor and the intern. The mentor's effort is usually rewarded by the positive environment resulting from interpersonal relations. Student teachers who work with cooperating teachers who take time to develop positive relationships will find their experience less stressful and more rewarding. A checklist for the mentor teacher to use in assessing her

Table 2.3.   Cooperating Teacher Checklist for Assessing Skills in Developing Positive Relationships with Student Teachers

	Proficient	Competent	Needs Work
1. I model appropriate teaching behaviors and strategies.			
2. I am able to explain the reasons for teaching decisions I make.			
3. I have a positive, professional attitude in dealing with students, colleagues, and parents.			
4. I demonstrate effective communication skills.			
5. I make expectations clear to the student teacher.			
6. I can build student teacher trust.			
7. I demonstrate positive regard for the student teacher.			
8. I am willing to share my classroom and students with another professional.			
9. I am willing to invest the time and effort it takes to develop positive relationships with my student teacher.			

skill in developing positive relationships with a student teacher is found in table 2.3.

NOTES

1. Joseph J. Caruso, "Cooperating Teacher and Student Teacher Phases of Development," *Young Children* 55, no. 1 (January 2000): 75–81.

2. Dian Yendol Silva, "Triad Journaling as a Tool for Reconceptualizing Supervision in the Professional Development School" (paper presented at the annual meeting of the American Educational Research Association, New Orleans, April 2000), 1–17.

3. James M. Kouzes and Barry Z. Posner, *Credibility: How Leaders Gain and Lose It, Why People Demand It* (San Francisco: Jossey-Bass, 1993), 1.

4. Tom Ganser, "The Contribution of Service as a Cooperating Teacher and Mentor Teacher to the Professional Development of Teachers" (paper presented at the annual meeting of the American Educational Research Association, Chicago, March 1997), 1–62.

5. Ganser, "The Contribution of Service as a Cooperating Teacher."

6. Stephen R. Covey, *The 7 Habits of Highly Effective People* (New York: Simon and Schuster, 1989), 235–60.

7. Lawrence Lyman and Harvey C. Foyle, *Cooperative Groupings for Interactive Learning: Students, Teachers, and Administrators* (Washington, D.C.: National Education Association, 1990), 59–60.

8. Lawrence Lyman, Alfred P. Wilson, C. Kent Garhart, Max O. Heim, and Wynona O. Winn, *Clinical Instruction and Supervision for Accountability* (Dubuque, Iowa: Kendall/Hunt, 1987), 106.

9. Susan K. Slick, "A University Supervisor Negotiates Territory and Status," *Journal of Teacher Education* 49, no. 4 (September–October 1998): 306–15.

10. Lawrence Lyman, Michael A. Morehead, and Harvey C. Foyle, "Building Teacher Trust in Supervision and Evaluation," *Illinois School Research and Development* 25, no. 2 (Winter 1989): 54–59.

CHAPTER 3

Student Teaching Program Assessment and Accountability

The student teaching experiences that a future teacher is involved in during his or her teacher preparation program are crucial to helping the future teacher acquire, practice, and enhance the skills needed to be successful in the classroom. The university must assure that a comprehensive program of assessment determines the future teacher's readiness to participate in each phase of the preparation program.

Assessment during the clinical experiences, which takes place before and during student teaching, provides the most important source of information about the future teacher's progress. Active involvement of trained mentor teachers in the assessment process improves the quantity and quality of feedback the future teacher receives, if mentors and university supervisor are well trained in their roles.

Since clinical field experiences are so important to the success of the future teacher, regular assessment of the student teaching program needs to occur to assure that the program is effective and accountable. Feedback from a variety of stakeholders, including students in the program, graduates of the program, mentor teachers, and employers of graduates of the program, needs to be analyzed on a systematic basis.

THE ROLE OF UNIVERSITY FACULTY

University faculty have the primary responsibility for assuring that future teachers meet the requirements of the teacher education program, appropriate subject matter standards, and state licensure standards.

Record keeping which assures that each candidate has met the requirements can be time-consuming and personnel-intensive. Having comprehensive data on each participant in the program is crucial for the accountability of the program and to meet accreditation and legal requirements.

Faculty who work with teacher candidates before they enter a teacher education program can provide important input about the knowledge, skills, and dispositions of students. Soliciting information from faculty members who teach courses required before admission to the program can assist the admissions committee in making appropriate decisions. A concern form, provided for the use of faculty, is a helpful tool in encouraging feedback from faculty who may have useful information from contact with students in their classes.

Since many future teachers complete some or all of their general education requirements at a community college, communication with community college instructors is also important. Community college partnerships, as discussed in the previous chapter, can provide opportunities for dialogue about future teachers. In the absence of such partnership agreements, regular meetings with instructors from community colleges with high numbers of transfer students to the university can be very helpful in making sure future teachers are ready for the teacher education program.

Teacher education and liberal arts faculty who work with future teachers in methods classes have a key role in assessment. Through contacts with future teachers, observation of interpersonal skills during class, conferences outside of class, and evaluation of course assignments, methods instructors gain vital insights about the skills of future teachers.

Regular meetings with methods teachers to discuss the progress of students in their classes provide important opportunities for formative assessment of the progress of candidates. Midterm meetings can identify students who are struggling in one or more classes. If a student is having difficulty in several classes and common problems or concerns are noted, the methods faculty may choose to meet with the candidate and discuss their concerns. Because meeting with a group of instructors can be intimidating, one or two instructors from the group may meet with students instead of the whole group of faculty.

At the conclusion of the semester when methods classes are taken, it is again useful to have the methods instructors meet to discuss the summative assessments of students in the program. It is helpful to have university supervisors who will be working with the students in clinical settings and appropriate representatives from the academic department and student teaching office attend these meetings so that they can identify potential concerns or problems with students they will be working with.

When problems and concerns have been identified during methods classes, a useful strategy is for the student teaching director, department chair, or other designee to meet with the future teacher and prepare a contract specifying the conditions for successful participation in the clinical experience. If punctuality and attendance have been problems in the methods classes, for example, the contract may specify a maximum number of absences or late arrivals permitted during the clinical experience. The contract may require the future teacher to contact the university supervisor in the event of any absence, late arrival, or early departure so that any potential problems in the clinical experience can be dealt with proactively.

During the student teaching experiences, the university supervisor or supervisors gather data about the performance of future teachers through regular observations, contacts with the student teacher, and contacts with the cooperating teachers. If both an academic and an education supervisor are assigned to a student teacher, it is important that they communicate together.

Alignment of schedules for observing the future teacher is one issue that academic and education supervisors can discuss. It is seldom helpful, for example, for two supervisors to visit the student teacher on the same day, and this issue can be avoided by communication. More importantly, if problems or concerns are noted in the performance of the student teacher, the supervisors can work together to provide the remediation needed to assist the student teacher.

THE ROLE OF THE COOPERATING TEACHER

The cooperating teacher has the best opportunity to assess the student teacher and provide helpful feedback because they are in daily contact.

The cooperating teacher also has in-depth understanding of the academic, social, and behavioral needs of the students in his or her class that the university supervisor will not have.

Because cooperating teachers have multiple roles, it is sometimes difficult for the cooperating teacher to find the time needed to provide feedback to the student teacher. Structuring the assessments in the student teaching program so that a weekly conference with the cooperating teacher and student teacher is required helps to assure that this important activity takes place.

The cooperating teacher also helps assess the quality of the planning, implementation, and assessment of instruction by the student teacher. Requiring at least one weekly formal assessment encourages the cooperating teacher and student teacher to meet regularly to discuss the student teacher's progress in teaching.

Cooperating teachers can also provide helpful feedback about the student teaching program and the quality of preparation of the student teachers they work with. It is important to involve cooperating teachers when discussing changes in the structure, classes, or assessments for the teacher education program as their input can be invaluable.

THE ROLE OF THE BUILDING PRINCIPAL

Like cooperating teachers, building principals have multiple roles to fulfill which can limit their availability to work with student teachers. Building principals can serve as another source of feedback to student teachers about their performance when invited to observe in the classroom and their schedules permit them to do so. As trained observers, principals can add to the information student teachers have about their teaching and give the student teacher experience in working with an administrator.

One of the advantages of working with student teachers in a professional development school setting is the opportunity for principals to observe candidates for potential teaching positions in the school or district. Interacting with student teachers in the actual school setting can help the administrator assess the suitability of the future teacher for the school or for other positions in the school district. Future teachers who are a good match for a school or district can be identified early and hired before they take positions elsewhere.

TRAINING FOR COOPERATING
TEACHERS AND UNIVERSITY SUPERVISORS

Working successfully with student teachers requires that both cooperating teachers and university supervisors have specific training. The ability to build a positive relationship with the student teacher, to help to plan and sequence the student teaching experience appropriately, and to supervise the student teacher, giving appropriate feedback and dealing with problems and concerns, are discussed in subsequent chapters of this book.

It is the responsibility of the university to assure that those who work with student teachers have the training needed to do so. University supervisors should be required to participate in a training program that provides them with information about the program, especially requirements for assessments. Opportunities to practice the required skills for successful supervision is another important attribute of a successful training program. It cannot be assumed that a faculty member who is knowledgeable in his or her discipline automatically has the skills needed to supervise student teachers effectively.

Appropriate training and ongoing support for cooperating teachers is also necessary.[1] As with the university supervisor, the training should focus on the requirements of the program and the skills needed for successful supervision of the student teacher. Ideally, successful completion of the training program would be required before a student teacher would be assigned to a cooperating teacher.

Incentives are needed to encourage busy university supervisors and cooperating teachers to participate in training. For the university supervisor, a stipend for travel may be appreciated. Stipends may also encourage participation by cooperating teachers. Providing university credit for cooperating teachers participating in the training program may also serve as an inducement to participate in training.

Designing training programs to assure that university supervisors and cooperating teachers have the skills needed to work effectively with student teachers requires an investment of both time and money. Faculty conducting the training will require compensation or load credit, in addition to the stipends paid for those attending the training sessions. However, the importance of assuring that every university supervisor and cooperating teacher has been specifically trained for their roles as supervisors cannot be overstated.

THE IMPORTANCE OF DISPOSITIONS

Since 2002, the National Council for Accreditation of Teacher Education has mandated that accredited teacher education programs identify and assess dispositions for successful teaching for future teachers. These dispositions are required as a part of the conceptual framework of the teacher education unit.[2]

Observing and assessing dispositions in future teachers needs to begin in general education classes. As stated earlier, general education faculty at the teacher education university and in community colleges can provide important information for assessment of the expected dispositions before the candidate is admitted to teacher education.

Communication about dispositions between cooperating teachers and university faculty is especially important because cooperating teachers can have an important influence on the way student teachers develop and demonstrate desired dispositions. Cooperating teachers and university faculty members need to work together to assure that the dispositions identified for assessment are appropriate and that the methods for assessing the dispositions are effective.[3]

Following are sample dispositions for assessment of initial program candidates:

- Candidates will demonstrate a commitment to professionalism and ethical standards.
- Candidates will demonstrate a desire to analyze concepts and clinical practices, to experiment, and to evaluate and/or initiate innovative practices.
- Candidates will demonstrate a dedication to lifelong learning by participating in professional organizations and keeping current with research in their field.

- Candidates will demonstrate a belief in having high expectations for all learners.
- Candidates will demonstrate a respect for cultural and individual differences by providing equitable learning opportunities for all.
- Candidates will demonstrate a desire to communicate with family and community members to make them partners in the educational process.
- Candidates will demonstrate a commitment to collaboration with other professionals to improve the overall learning of students.

Source: The Teachers College, Emporia State University

SELF-ASSESSMENT

Future teachers must have the capability and desire to assess their teaching performance on an ongoing basis. Using data from planning, teaching, and student assessment, future teachers need to be able to identify what is going well and to identify and implement appropriate changes as needed.

As the future teacher begins working with students, part of the assessment of his or her work needs to include appropriate self-assessment. An important part of self-assessment is to help the student teacher identify areas of needed improvement and to develop strategies for working toward those improvements. In their postgraduation assignments in their own classrooms, future teachers will need to be proactive, not waiting for feedback to monitor and adjust their teaching.

Future teachers also need to be able to identify specific strengths they have in the classroom. Often, the solution to an instructional problem can be found by looking at what the future teacher does well and capitalizing on these strengths.

In the supervisory process outlined in chapter 4 of this book, conferences with the student teacher are at first primarily planned and conducted by cooperating teachers and university supervisors. As the student teaching experience continues, one of the measures of the professional growth of the student teacher is his or her ability to analyze teaching performance with progressively less assistance from supervisors.

TEACHER WORK SAMPLES

Teacher work samples can provide evidence of the student teacher's ability to plan, teach, and assess while meeting expected standards. A teacher work sample can be defined as "an exhibit of teaching performance that provides direct evidence" of the student teacher's competence in instructional planning, implementation, and assessment.[4]

The Renaissance Group of teacher education colleges has developed a model for teacher work samples that requires the student teacher to provide evidence of accountability for the learning of the students he or she is working with. In the Renaissance Teacher Work Sample model, teaching performance standards with indicators are specified. Prompts, teaching tasks, and rubrics are provided to assist the student teacher as he or she develops the teacher work sample. A scoring rubric for each task is provided. The outcomes of the teacher work sample must be aligned with state or local standards and the student teacher must analyze the student learning that took place by comparing pretest and posttest data from the students in the class he or she is teaching.

At Emporia State University, teacher work samples are "blind" evaluated by trained evaluators. Evaluators may be cooperating teachers, administrators, or university faculty. A cooperating teacher or university faculty member may not evaluate the work sample of a student teacher they have worked with. Factors measured by teacher work sample assessment include:

- Contextual Information and Learning Environment
- Unit Goals and Objectives
- Instructional Design and Implementation
- Demonstration of Integration Skills
- Analysis of Classroom Learning Environment
- Analysis of Assessment Procedures
- Reflection and Self-Evaluation

Source: The Teachers College, Emporia State University

Training on the teacher work sample process is a necessary part of the training provided to cooperating teachers and university supervisors. Professionals working with student teachers need to be able to provide appropriate assistance to student teachers without helping them too much.

Evaluators of the teacher work samples need additional training to be able to assess the teacher work sample fairly and to assure inter-rater reliability. As with training for supervision, teacher work sample training requires a willingness to expend time and funding. The teacher work sample provides important performance-based evidence of the student teacher's impact on student learning which justifies the necessary time and expense.

ACCOUNTABILITY THROUGH ASSESSMENT

Calls for teacher education programs to be more accountable for the performance of future teachers are intensifying.[5] One of the ways teacher education programs can demonstrate their effectiveness is through the assessment data collected during the preparation of future teachers.

Most teacher education programs collect a great deal of data about their students. It is important to analyze that data cooperatively, with other stakeholders as well as members of the university staff, to identify strengths and weaknesses of the teacher education program and to assure that a meaningful student teacher experience is provided for all candidates.

It is also important that assessments be aligned with the conceptual framework of the college. In the student teaching program, for example, assessment forms need to reflect the specific competencies and skills expected of the student teacher. Ideally, multiple assessments of program standards, at various stages of the teacher education program, will demonstrate the achievement of future teachers.

Cooperating teachers and university supervisors as well as student teachers can provide important feedback about the usefulness of student teaching assessment forms. Terminology, format, or rating scales may be confusing or unclear. With regular feedback from supervisors and candidates, the quality of the feedback provided to the student teacher can be assured.

ACCOUNTABILITY THROUGH SHARED GOVERNANCE

Sharing the responsibility for governance, oversight, and assessment of teacher education can be facilitated by creating shared governance councils. P–12 teachers and administrators may meet on a regular basis with university teachers and administrators to discuss the progress of shared teacher education efforts. Education faculty members and administrators may meet on a regular basis with their liberal arts and sciences colleagues to discuss the curriculum and assessment of the teacher education curriculum.

When a large number of teacher education students are placed in a school district as freshman and sophomore observers and tutors, as juniors working with small groups of students under university faculty supervision, and as seniors working as student teachers, a "teacher council" may be created with membership from P–12 school cooperating teachers and administrators and university teachers and administrators. Goals of such a council can include: coordination of dates for beginning and ending placement experiences, discussion of assessments, identification of concerns and problems, and celebration of successful efforts in preparing future teachers.

To coordinate the efforts of liberal arts and science faculty and education faculty working with teacher education students, a "teacher education council" may be useful. Each department involved in the preparation of future teachers has representation on the council. Among the responsibilities of the council are: providing input about proposed teacher education curricular changes, analyzing admission requirements and assessments of teacher education students, and celebrating successful efforts in preparing future teachers.

As partnerships with community colleges are developed, shared governance councils are also useful. Representatives from each of the stakeholder groups involved in the partnership should meet together on a regular basis to assure that the goals of the partnership are being met.

ACCOUNTABILITY THROUGH EVALUATION

An important part of the assessment of the student teaching program comes from stakeholders in the program. Feedback from instructors, cooperating teachers, and university supervisors should be systematically collected and analyzed to determine the strengths and needs of the program. While collecting and analyzing data from stakeholders is time-consuming, the quality of the student teaching program depends on this feedback.

Feedback from graduates of the teacher education program and from administrators who have employed graduates as teachers is another source of valuable evidence of the effectiveness of the teacher education program. When professional development school models are utilized, the feedback from employers is ongoing as schools and districts participating in professional development school programs often hire graduates to teach in their own schools (see table 3.1).

One of the measures of effectiveness to consider is the rate of attrition of graduates of the program. After three years, how many graduates have left the teaching profession? After five years, how many graduates have left the teaching profession? The substantial effort and

Table 3.1.   Intern/Mentor Teacher/Principal Evaluation of the PDS Coordinator

Coordinator _____ Date _____						
PDS Site _____ (Circle one)	Intern	Mentor Teacher			Principal	
	Low			High		No info
1. Clearly communicates program and outcomes for the PDS to mentor teachers and building administrator	1	2	3	4	5	NI
2. Provides monthly calendars	1	2	3	4	5	NI
3. Works effectively one-on-one to answer	1	2	3	4	5	NI
4. Is available for consultation by appointment and/or by e-mail	1	2	3	4	5	NI
5. Relates well to building-level administration	1	2	3	4	5	NI
6. Displays effective listening and communication skills	1	2	3	4	5	NI
7. Provides appropriate feedback to interns	1	2	3	4	5	NI
8. Willing to schedule mentor meetings as requested	1	2	3	4	5	NI
9. Works cooperatively with mentor teachers	1	2	3	4	5	NI

What has your coordinator done well in her or his performance as a coordinator of the professional development school?

How could your coordinator improve her or his performance as a coordinator of the professional development school?

Please make any additional comments you feel would be helpful. You may use the back of this sheet if needed.

**A copy of this evaluation will be given to the site coordinator.
Source: Department of Early Childhood/Elementary Teacher Education, Emporia State Univ.

expense on the part of future teachers dictates that their success in the classroom be a measure of accountability for teacher education programs.

CHAPTER SUMMARY

As outlined in this chapter, assessment data for student teachers includes feedback from general education course instructors as well as feedback and performance assessments from methods course instructors. Teacher work samples offer promise as a performance assessment for documenting the impact of the student teacher on the learning of students. Formative and summative assessment by trained university supervisors and cooperating teachers is the best assurance of the competence of the student teacher.

Almost all teacher education programs collect a great deal of data about their candidates. The challenge is to utilize the data systematically to improve the quality of the program. This is especially important in the area of student teaching and other field experiences. In student teaching, not only is the learning of the student teacher involved, but the learning of P–12 students can be impacted positively or negatively by the involvement of student teachers in the classroom.

NOTES

1. Grace Rubenstein, "Building a Better Teacher: Confronting the Crisis in Teacher Training" (2007). Retrieved January 8, 2008, from www.edutopia .org/node/4992/print.

2. National Council for Accreditation of Teacher Education, *Professional Standards for the Accreditation of Schools, Colleges, and Departments of Education* (Washington, D.C.: National Council for Accreditation of Teacher Education, 2002).

3. J. F. Voneschenbach and W. B. Gile, "Dispositions for Teacher Education Candidates," *School-University Partnerships* 1, no. 1 (2007): 72–79.

4. Renaissance Partnership Project, "Renaissance Teacher Work Samples." Retrieved January 14, 2008, from www.uni.edu/itq/RTWS/index/htm.

5. Arthur Levine, *Educating School Teachers* (Washington, D.C.: The Education Schools Project, 2006).

CHAPTER 4

Planning and Sequencing

Planning and organizing the student teacher's time in the classroom is a crucial element in providing opportunities for success. When a mentor demonstrates time management and instructional planning skills, these experiences are much easier for the intern to learn. Following a specific plan for sequencing the student teaching experience helps ensure that an intern's time in the assignment will be beneficial.

TIME MANAGEMENT

One of the most challenging elements in teaching is time management.[1] Teachers are expected to manage an instructional program with ever-increasing content and expectations, relate positively with students, communicate effectively with parents, and serve as collegial members of school improvement teams. Teachers also need to balance out-of-school responsibilities such as family and friends.

For these reasons, deciding to become a mentor and adding additional responsibilities to an already challenging load needs to be made with care. Potential cooperating teachers who already feel they are "stretched to the limit" must think carefully about accepting the responsibility of working with an intern. Although interns are often able to provide valuable assistance in the classroom, developing a positive, professional relationship with the student teacher, planning and organizing her experiences in the classroom, and supervising can require a significant commitment of time.

Although the amount of time available to mentors is limited, the ways in which the time is utilized are not. Some strategies for effective time management include organizing, prioritizing, reducing paperwork, and taking time for relaxation and reflection. Considerable teaching time can be lost when organization is lacking. For example, poor filing systems can make it difficult to retrieve needed materials quickly. Keeping track of current and future commitments with a frequently updated calendar helps the teacher anticipate and schedule appropriately. Modeling this for an intern can save him valuable time in future professional activities. Teachers who do not utilize effective strategies for organizing information and tasks may feel even more frustrated when adding the demands of working with an intern.

Prioritizing is another time-management skill required of teachers. It is important that students in the classroom are the mentor's first priority. Basic responsibilities are not always discretionary, but accepting other tasks such as committee assignments, extracurricular duties, and community projects should be considered carefully. In addition, teachers must also find time for family, friends, and personal commitments. Helping an intern recognize the importance of weighing outside commitments carefully during teaching should be part of the professional experience.

A problem for many teachers is effectively dealing with significant amounts of paperwork required by a multitude of agencies, government regulations, district and building expectations, and student record keeping. One suggestion is to look for ways to reduce the number of papers that the teacher deals with, such as the amount of paperwork submitted by students. It is certainly important to check for student understanding frequently, but this does not always require the completion of a paper-and-pencil task that must be graded. Checking for understanding while students are working in class and assessing students in different ways can reduce the number of papers and still provide needed feedback to students about their performance. Most effective teachers develop grading systems that allow flexibility for reviewing student work. Modeling this for a student teacher is essential. Time management strategies *must* be discussed throughout an intern's experience.

A concern for many teachers is the overwhelming amount of information received via district, state, regional, and national reporting agencies and electronic mail. Although some of these reports and messages are important, working to reduce unwanted and useless information can be time-saving.

Although it may seem contradictory to suggest time for reflection and relaxation as strategies for time management, teachers who do not engage in these important activities will usually be less productive. All teachers need time to reflect about their teaching and other important personal things. Such reflection helps teachers prioritize and maintain a positive, constructive attitude toward their profession.[2] Part of every student teaching program will require professional and personal reflection by the intern. Cooperating teachers who demonstrate reflection will foster that behavior by the intern. Time for relaxation, including appropriate wellness activities such as exercise, help the teacher maintain the focus and balance essential for successful interactions with students and other colleagues.

As in many other areas, mentor teachers serve as a positive or negative example for interns in the area of time management. Mentors who manage time effectively demonstrate appropriate practices that interns may emulate as a professional.

INSTRUCTIONAL PLANNING

Effective instructional planning is a hallmark of excellent teaching. Since the historical trend in education has been to add requirements to curriculum without subtracting other content, teachers are faced with incredible responsibilities today. Educational goals, standards, and levels of accountability have multiplied almost exponentially at national, state, and local levels. At the same time, the inclusion of students with wide-ranging academic and social needs makes the teaching of an expanded curriculum even more challenging.[3]

Long-range planning by teachers helps ensure that required curriculum outcomes can be addressed in the classroom. The cooperating teacher's philosophy, classroom rules, procedures and routines, and arrangement of the classroom must be carefully considered by good teachers and become the foundation for curriculum planning and implementation.[4] Because the student teacher will not know how these important elements of planning were established, the mentor must outline and describe reasons for these basic planning decisions.

In order to work with a student teacher effectively, the mentor must carefully analyze the required curriculum outcomes of the grade level and subject areas. Developing a long-range instructional plan for meeting these objectives throughout the academic year is necessary. An effective long-range plan includes a timeline for working on outcomes in each subject area. Curriculum materials, including textbooks and other resources used in achieving positive outcomes, should also be identified. Dates for mandated district and state testing and times for reviewing need to be noted as part of the long-term planning process.[5] Sharing these strategies with interns will assist them in present and future instructional planning.

Once planning decisions have been made, the mentor teacher and intern can identify specific content and outcomes each will be responsible for. Once the student teacher becomes familiar with required content, formulating appropriate plans for instruction and identifying additional resources for teaching can occur. Often, beginning educators struggle with deciding what important topics or concepts to teach. The mentors can assist in guiding the intern's selection of content in the early stages of the experience.

While the student teacher benefits from appropriate long-range planning by the mentor, the real beneficiaries are the students in the classroom. Long-range planning can facilitate a smooth transition from the cooperating teacher's instruction to the student teacher's. Another smooth transition will occur when the mentor resumes responsibility for instruction. Effective planning and implementation ensures that students have the best opportunities possible to learn, regardless of who is teaching.

SEQUENCING THE STUDENT TEACHING EXPERIENCE

Beginning the Experience

At the beginning of the student teaching experience, the cooperating teacher has three important tasks: getting acquainted with the intern; sharing expectations, philosophy, and concerns; and sharing necessary information about the school, classroom, and students. The student teacher will be anxious to know these things. By sharing the above-mentioned information with the intern, the acclimation and transition into teaching will be more successful.

Foyle, Morehead, and Lyman have identified five key behaviors of mentors that can assist student teachers in the beginning of their experience. These behaviors are friendliness, openness, warm regard, listening, and empathy.[6] Several of these behaviors were discussed in chapter 2, "Building Positive Relationships."

By encouraging the student teacher to share appropriate personal and professional information, the mentor demonstrates friendliness and warm regard. Suggestions for personal and professional discussion items can be found in table 4.1. Being interested in the intern's background and experiences and anxious to utilize skills of the student teacher in the classroom is also important.

Several issues need to be discussed with the student teacher early in the experience. Taking time to clarify expectations, rules, and procedures helps prevent confusion and frustration. A list of important issues to discuss can be found in chapters 1 and 3. Materials such as the school handbook can provide helpful supplemental information. It is especially important that the student teacher clearly understand discipline, confidentiality, and reporting policies before working with students.

Table 4.1.   Beginning Conferences with Student Teachers

Things to Ask the Student Teacher

1. Ask about the student teacher's personal and professional background.
2. Ask the student teacher why he or she chose teaching for a profession.
3. Ask about previous experiences with children.
4. Ask what his or her biggest fear or concern is.
5. Ask what his or her strengths are.
6. Ask about high school and college activities and favorite subjects.
7. Ask about hobbies and interests.
8. Ask what subject or subjects he or she would like to teach first.
9. Ask if the student teacher has any questions or concerns and encourage the student teacher to ask questions as they come up.

These suggestions are adapted from the videotape *Conferencing with Student Teachers: The Beginning Conference* by Harvey Foyle, Michael Morehead, and Lawrence Lyman (New York: Insight Media, 1992). Used with permission.

Table 4.2.   Topics to Cover in Initial Conferences

1. Share personal and professional background information.
2. Share philosophy and expectations. Be sure to mention pet peeves.
3. Clarify expectations for dress, arrival time, confidentiality, reporting of child abuse, and school and classroom rules and procedures.
4. Take the student teacher on a tour of the school and introduce the student teacher to colleagues, the principal, secretary, appropriate support personnel, and custodians during the first week he or she is in the building.
5. Discuss classroom management procedures and expectations for the student teacher with respect to discipline.
6. Discuss activities for the first two weeks of school.
7. Develop a schedule for teaching and for conferencing with the student teacher.
8. Give a brief overview of what is known about students the student teacher will be working with. Do not share negative information at this time.
9. Discuss lesson planning requirements and dates on which plans are due.

Early conferences with the student teacher will primarily be directed by the mentor. Although the cooperating teacher should encourage the intern to share information and ask questions, it is important that the mentor make expectations and necessary information clear to the student teacher (see table 4.2). Clarifying expectations about minor issues early in the experience (e.g., punctuality, attendance) allows both parties the opportunity to discuss more significant issues later. The university supervisor can assist both the mentor and intern in the first week and outline topics to discuss.

During the first meeting with the student teacher and mentor, the university supervisor should verify that the intern has met all the requirements for the placement and that the mentor has all of the necessary information from the university. By making an introductory visit early in the assignment, the supervisor ensures that the placement of the student teacher is appropriate and that the mentor and intern have information needed regarding the assignment. It is important that both the student and the cooperating teacher receive information on how to contact the supervisor. A date for the next visit should be identified and a tentative schedule for all visits by the supervisor discussed. The university supervisor also needs to share expectations for the student teacher, especially in the areas of lesson planning, attendance, substituting, and professional behavior.

During the first two weeks in the classroom, mentors should provide opportunities for guided observation of the students. Guided observation helps the intern becomes familiar with the students and classroom while settling in. A guide for classroom observation, such as the one found in table 4.3, can provide specific things for the student teacher for look for.

Taking time to review the intern's observations during a weekly conference can help mentors evaluate important factors such as an intern's perceptions of the classroom and students. Additionally, cooperating teachers can determine if the intern has made accurate observations and

Table 4.3.   Classroom Observation Guide

During the first two weeks of school, most student teachers benefit from guided observation tasks, which help them become oriented to the students, teacher, and classroom. The student teacher should observe and interact with students as directed by the mentor teacher and answer as many of the questions as possible. When the student teacher has completed the observation process, the student teacher and mentor teacher should conference to determine the accuracy of the student teacher's observations and conclusions.

1. How does the mentor teacher make students feel welcome on the first day of class? How does the mentor teacher involve students during the first week of class so that students feel as though they are a part of the class?
2. How does the mentor teacher reduce student anxiety and fear during the first days of class?
3. How does the teacher get to know students before they arrive in class and during the first days of class?
4. What are the classroom and school rules for students? What is the role of the student teacher in classroom discipline and management?
5. How does the mentor teacher positively reinforce desired student behaviors in the classroom?
6. How does the mentor teacher check to make sure that students understand what has been taught?
7. How are groups established? Why does the mentor teacher group students?
8. Which students appear to be leaders in the classroom? How do you know?
9. Which students have good verbal skills? How do you know?
10. Which students seem to learn quickly and easily? How do you know?
11. Which students appear to be socially skilled in the classroom? How do you know?
12. Which students appear to be shy and reticent? How do you know?
13. Which students appear to have difficulty getting along with others? How do you know?
14. Which students need extra help to understand and participate appropriately? All the time or only in certain subjects? What do these students do when they are frustrated? How do you know?
15. Which students appear to need more attention (positive or negative) from the mentor teacher and the student teacher than others? How do these students get the attention they want? How do they react if they do not get the attention they want? How do you know?
16. What other interesting or unexpected things have been observed?

has "with-it-ness."[7] Observations made by the student teacher that differ from those of the mentor can facilitate discussion and allow for clarification. Occasionally, the discussion of the observation guide can alert the mentor that an intern has made errors in observing or interacting with students during the initial days of the assignment. Discussing the observations early in an experience may assist the mentor in pointing out the potential challenges for the student teacher and possibly alleviate potential problems. If concerns arise, it is appropriate to visit with the university supervisor to clarify questions and concerns. If an intern is not aware of students' interactions, behaviors, and attentiveness, serious classroom management issues could emerge later.

Another appropriate task for the student teacher during the first two weeks of the assignment is to briefly interview students in the class. (At the secondary level, it might be just a few students in each class.) A list of possible interview questions can be found in the following paragraph. These brief interviews can help the student teacher gain valuable information about the personalities, learning styles, and interests of students. Mentors should encourage interns to share any interesting or unexpected things discovered during the interviews. This information can be valuable to the mentor as well. Interviews will also enhance the interpersonal relations of an intern with students in the class.

Few student teachers will be satisfied by only observing and interviewing during the first two weeks of their assignments. Cooperating teachers should provide opportunities for interns to assume responsibility for routine classroom tasks, such as taking attendance, completing calendar activities, reading to students, or working with small groups. A simple project at the elementary level, such as creating a bulletin board of self-portraits created by students in the class, can be satisfying. At the secondary level, developing a unit plan related to future teaching might be appropriate.

The approach mentors use when introducing the student teacher to the class can be an important factor in determining success. By presenting the intern to the students as a teacher rather than a "student" teacher, the mentor signals it is expected that the class treat the intern with the same respect accorded all teachers. The mentor must also let parents know there is another teacher working in the classroom. Parents may be curious or concerned if their child tells them about a student teacher they were unaware of. (This is especially significant for elementary classrooms.)

It is important during the first two weeks of the student teaching assignment to have a brief, daily conference. This brief conference provides an opportunity for the student teacher to ask questions or express concerns or frustrations. It is important to encourage the intern to ask questions about routines in the classroom, student behavior and attitudes, and the mentor's instructional and behavior decisions. If the student teacher is reluctant to ask questions and does not seem to be able to analyze the classroom, students, and teaching, this may be a concern to share with the university supervisor.

Possible structured interview questions for student teachers to use with students:

1. Tell me about your family. Brothers and sisters? Pets?
2. Have you always lived here? What other places have you lived?
3. What are you good at?
4. What is your favorite subject in school?
5. What gives you the most trouble in school?
6. What are you looking forward to this year?
7. What are you nervous about this year?
8. What do you like to do outside of school?
9. What is the best book you ever read?
10. What do you think makes somebody a good teacher?

Daily conferences also allow the mentor an opportunity to clarify expectations and deal directly with any issues that might be of concern, such as an intern not being punctual or completing assigned tasks in a timely manner. Conferences early in the semester will give the cooperating teacher an opportunity to address these concerns before they become problematic.

Getting the Student Teacher More Involved in the Classroom

By the third week, most student teachers are ready to take over at least one subject area. As part of the plan, the mentor will usually encourage a student teacher to assume these responsibilities. In a middle school or secondary assignment, the student teacher may work with a particular class period. Sometimes interns are given too much responsibility too early. The old model of "sink or swim" is not acceptable. If an assigned mentor leaves an intern on her own after only a week, the mentor is not meeting his professional responsibilities and his action borders on professional malpractice.

Some student teachers need a little more time to adjust to the classroom before assuming responsibilities for the whole class. These interns may benefit from working with a small group of students first, such as a reading group in an elementary classroom. Middle and high school interns may work with cooperative groups to help students with problems or answer questions. These types of introductory activities are appropriate for all interns, but some will take longer to become acclimated to an experience. Professional judgment of the mentor is essential in this first phase and can have a significant impact on future success.

Planning for additional responsibilities should be done collaboratively and take place during the second week. Involving the university supervisor at this juncture is essential. Each week thereafter should include a discussion of future responsibilities to be assumed by the student teacher. During this time, it is usually helpful for the mentor to carefully review the written plans for teaching with the intern and outline expectations for planning and implementing. If possible, the mentor should model the first lesson and then permit the intern to teach a second, similar lesson to the class.

As the intern begins to have direct responsibility for planning and teaching, it is important for the mentor to be in the classroom. This provides an opportunity to note examples of positive communication with students, appropriate instructional practices, and good management strategies as they are observed. These desired behaviors can be reinforced in a brief, daily conference. This feedback in the early stages will be beneficial for both participants. First, trust will be enhanced by this communication. Second, clarification of expectations by the mentor related to instruction will enhance the intern's performance. Finally, it should quicken the implementation of effective classroom management strategies for the intern.

It is also important for the mentor to record any concerns or changes the intern should make while teaching. Specific suggestions for change should be given before the intern works with the students again. If a mentor observes that the student teacher successfully incorporates suggestions into future instruction, it is especially important to reinforce the practice.

Based on the student teacher's progress, additional subject areas or academic periods should be added to her responsibilities so she can plan and implement instructions as a full-time teacher. The length of full-time teaching is often negotiable and can vary from three to eight weeks. Most mentors are reluctant to give up their class for a significant period of time, but interns need at least three weeks of full-time teaching. Every student teacher needs time to be in full control of the class without interruption from a mentor. During a full sixteen-week semester, a two- to four-week period should be sufficient. Early in the experience, the intern should use the cooperating teacher's materials and lessons. If the cooperating teacher is concerned that the intern is not progressing as expected, it is essential to confer with the university supervisor. By notifying the supervisor, his input and expertise can be utilized if it becomes necessary to make changes to the student teaching experience.

From the third week of the assignment until the midpoint, the student teacher should be accepting additional responsibilities for planning and teaching. The mentor should be giving less specific feedback about lesson plans as the student teacher evidences the ability to plan more appropriately. More sophisticated types of analysis should begin taking place as well. For example, comparing interaction with males/females, monitoring levels of questions, or reflecting on student learning should emerge.

A concern often observed at this stage of the student teaching experience is time and stress management. As an intern assumes more responsibility for planning and instruction, it is common for him or her to feel overwhelmed and anxious about the responsibilities assumed and even to feel inadequate. These feelings may come from the intern's ongoing comparison or himself or herself to the cooperating teacher or other master teachers.[8] Positive and specific reinforcement from the mentor will help relieve anxiety. Using affirmation statements as discussed in chapter 2 will reassure the intern that the mentor has confidence in her abilities.

As the student teacher assumes increasing responsibility in the classroom, lessons should be observed to assess how the intern is handling classroom management. An intern's awareness of student misbehavior, ability to anticipate problems before they occur, and use of positive, effective strategies to deal with minor behavior problems should be observed. Observations and suggestions about classroom management must be shared using weekly conferences or more often as necessary. During the early stages of an assignment, it is essential to identify and offer suggestions related to classroom environment and management. It is important not to leave the intern alone in the classroom for more than brief periods of time until the mentor is convinced he can handle discipline effectively.

Student teachers should also be gaining skill in instructional planning, teaching, and assessment. Specific feedback about teaching decisions discussed in chapter 5 ("Supervising the Student Teacher") needs to be given on a daily basis or in the weekly conference. Some mentors prefer to write a brief note to the student teacher after observing a lesson to identify what has gone well and what should be changed. This strategy can provide prompt feedback to the student teacher and furnish a record of the strengths and weaknesses that can be shared with a university supervisor during her visit to the classroom. All feedback needs to be specific and focus on one or two key themes. Discussing more than one or two issues can seem overwhelming to the intern. Also, determining which topics are most important to review can be difficult when there are multiple concerns.

The Midpoint Assessment

The midpoint of the student teacher's experience should be marked by a summative evaluation of strengths and weaknesses. Most universities require that a university supervisor be part of the midpoint conference and that a summative evaluation be completed and discussed with the student teacher. At the midpoint, the university may also request that the mentor assign a letter grade to the student teacher's progress to date. At this time, in fairness to all parties, it is expected that any serious concerns be shared with the intern. Due process and general, professional expectations warrant such disclosure during the midpoint assessment.

Not overrating the progress of the student teacher at this point in the experience is important. Strengths will, of course, be discussed, with specific examples so the intern can continue to grow professionally. It is also important, however, to help the student teacher set goals for improvement during the remainder of the experience. Even when the student teacher is making exemplary progress, a plan to continue professional growth and development is essential. Suggestions for helping outstanding interns may be found in chapter 8 ("The Excellent Student Teacher").

With some interns, concerns at this midpoint may be serious enough to require university supervision in this summative conference. When mentors believe serious concerns exist, cooperating teachers *must* involve the university supervisor in the midterm evaluation. The university supervisor can assist in formulating a specific plan for improvement. Additional information for dealing with student teachers who are experiencing difficulties can be found in chapter 7 ("The Incompetent Student Teacher").

Discussing any weaknesses during the summative midterm conference can influence the intern's future attitude toward supervisors. Most importantly, the issue of trust and a sense of respect can be impacted negatively. If identified weaknesses are substantive, in order to ensure trust, openness, and continued respect, supervisors must reaffirm their belief in the potential success of the intern.

Cooperating teachers should make sure that interns have a clear understanding of the mentor's assessment of their progress to date and clearly understand the expectations for improvement during the final portion of the assignment. By being clear about concerns or problems at this time, the intern has an opportunity to improve so the summative conference at the end can be more positive and the overall experience more successful.

Sometime during this midpoint, a substantive transition should begin to emerge in an intern's professional growth. As conferences continue, a student teacher who is maturing professionally should be moving from a survival mode to a role as "teacher." This can best be determined by listening to the student teacher's comments about teaching and observing his interactions with students. The focus should now be on "learning and needs of children" and not on the interns themselves.[9] If this occurs, the remainder of the semester should be professionally productive. If the focus on children is not evident, then this is a serious indication that an intern's professional growth is not occurring adequately. The university supervisor and cooperating teacher must confer and ensure they are in agreement about this observation. If they are, then corrective action should be taken immediately.

The Final Weeks of the Student Teaching Experience

During the second half of the experience, most interns will continue to assume more responsibility for planning and teaching in the classroom. During the final weeks of the experience, the mentor's weekly conference strategies with the student teacher will usually change. In the early weeks of an assignment, mentors are usually directive, providing specific reinforcement and suggestions for modification of teaching as appropriate. Later in the experience, mentors will encourage interns to take a more active part in weekly conferences.[10] Clarification and brainstorming strategies will require an intern to analyze her performance and facilitate more interaction with the mentor. The goal of conferences with competent and excellent student teachers is to cause more reflection about their teaching.[11] Student teachers need to identify what is going well, as well as identify problems and suggest possible solutions. This process of reflection is an integral part of professional growth necessary for success of the intern.

Weekly formative conferences with the student teacher should focus on refining instructional strategies, utilizing varied methods of assessment, and anticipating problems that may occur. Written lesson plans may be less detailed if the intern has evidenced the ability to plan appropriately, yet it is important to discuss short- and long-term goals, as well as ensure all students are being taught effectively. By this time, pacing of lessons and an ability to determine how quickly students complete assignments should be an acquired skill. If the intern is still having difficulty with these issues, comprehensive daily planning may still be required.

An important strategy to assist in evaluation performance is the use of videotape. Some student teachers balk at the idea of videotaping because they feel uncomfortable watching themselves. However, there are few better techniques for any educator to get realistic feedback on strengths and weaknesses related to the teaching process. Mentors may give an intern the choice of viewing the videotape privately or with the mentor present. Some may elect to watch the first videotaped episode by themselves; this is not uncommon and allows an individual a private opportunity to reflect. Later, when taped episodes are viewed together, cooperating teachers can assure the intern that both strengths and weaknesses are being observed and discussed. Videotapes made throughout the experience can provide feedback about nonverbal cues, movement in the classroom, possible behaviors missed, inconsistency in feedback, and professional teaching growth. Some school districts request a videotape of new teachers as part of the application process, so it is important to make sure this experience is made available.

As mentioned earlier, the focus of the student teacher usually changes as the experience progresses. At the beginning, most interns tend to focus on themselves and what they are doing. Sharing personal feelings and reactions at this time is most important when visiting with the mentor. With most competent and excellent interns, this self-centered focus will change during the student teaching experience. The focus changes from being preoccupied with how they are doing to what is happening and how the students are reacting to instructions. This may be one of the best informal assessments of the student teacher's readiness for his own classroom. To observe this change in focus is an excellent indication that appropriate professional growth is transpiring.

Concluding the Experience

One important experience to make available is an opportunity to participate in conferences with parents. Numerous studies conducted by Morehead indicate that first-year teachers feel inadequate in their preparation relating to issues concerning parents and parent-teacher conferences. Depending on the competence and confidence of the student teacher, the mentor may allow the intern to take the lead in some of the conferences. Before conferences occur, goals and appropriate methods used to share information should be discussed, and a plan for the meeting with parents should be reviewed. It is especially important for the student teacher to learn ways to deal with difficult parents in a positive, professional manner. Appropriate modeling by the mentor should occur first, and the opportunity to lead a few parent-teacher conferences is necessary. The mentor and other teachers should be present to assist the student teacher and help with any potential problems. Role-playing might be good preparation after the first few conferences so that an intern can iron out minor flaws without fear of being ineffective. Reminding an intern that each parent conference should start with a positive comment and focus on only one or two key issues at a time will go a long way toward ensuring future success.

Inviting a building administrator to visit while an intern is teaching is also an activity that can assist professional growth. A principal or assistant principal will provide valuable feedback about teaching and other important professional issues. More information on ways the administrator can help student teachers can be found in chapter 9 ("The Principal's Role").

As the experience concludes, planning for a smooth transition of the mentor's return to teaching should occur. It is usually helpful for the student teacher to "give back" responsibility for teaching subjects or academic periods as they were assigned. By the final week of an experience, the student teacher may be responsible, as she was earlier in the experience, for only one or two subject areas of academic periods.

At the conclusion of the experience, the cooperating teacher has several important tasks. First, having a summative evaluation conference reviewing the student teacher's progress and assigning a grade will be necessary. Most universities will ask mentors to complete a final evaluation form. Additionally, a mentor will be asked by the student teacher to complete a reference letter for a placement file, which will be sent to a university placement office. Mentors sometimes find it difficult to write an appropriate reference for the student teacher's career placement file. It is important to remember that these two forms serve different purposes. Recommendation letters are just that, and should focus on the positive. If serious weaknesses exist, professional responsibility requires mention of those weaknesses. The final university evaluation should focus on successes but is intended to help the intern grow professionally and should indicate areas for improvement.

The following are suggestions that may be used for writing evaluations of student teachers and for cooperating teachers in writing references for interns.

Four Paragraph Format:

    Paragraph 1: Sentence summarizing student teacher assignment. Sentences describing characteristics and traits, such as enthusiasm, creativity, willingness to work hard, rapport with students, staff, and parents

    Paragraph 2: Sentences describing planning and organizational skills, ability to evaluate effectively, ability to use a variety of methods and strategies, develop and implement appropriate instructional objectives

    Paragraph 3: Sentences describing ability to motivate and manage students, ability to keep students interested and involved, provide for individual student differences

    Paragraph 4: Overall summary of the student teaching assignment, prediction for success of student teacher in full-time teaching

The following examples can be helpful in qualifying statements.

Qualifying Words:

usually	often
sometimes	occasionally
may	with (conditions)
probably	shows the potential to

Qualifying Statements:

    Strong Performance: Miss Smith demonstrated excellent rapport with students.

Qualified Statement: Miss Smith usually demonstrated excellent rapport with students.

Strong Performance: Miss Smith managed incidents of classroom misbehavior appropriately and fairly.

Qualified Statement: Miss Smith often managed incidents of classroom misbehavior appropriately and fairly.

Strong Performance: Miss Smith will do well in future teaching.

Qualified Statement: Miss Smith may do well in future teaching. Miss Smith may do well in future teaching if provided with strong guidance and supervision.

The following descriptive words can be used when developing reference letters or writing final evaluations for that university.

Excellent Performance	*Good Performance*
extraordinary	good
excellent	capable
distinguished	competent
superb	effective
exceptional	appropriate
special	proper
superior	favorable
noteworthy	above average
notable	positive
extensive	productive
outstanding	

Fair Performance	*Poor Performance*
adequate	below standard
sufficient	unprepared
suitable	inadequate
fair	weak
satisfactory	unqualified
acceptable	unacceptable
average	unfit
passable	inappropriate
ordinary	

The ending conference in most situations is a celebration of a job well done. Unlike the first conferences, which were controlled primarily by the mentor, the final conference should be a professional dialogue about teaching. The intern should be encouraged to reflect on what went well during the experience and how those strengths may be used in future teaching. Encouraging a student teacher to reflect on highlights of the semester and things she finds most memorable helps promote the celebration.

In a final conference, open-ended questions help ensure that the intern is an active participant in the conference. As the experience concludes, interns should be encouraged to analyze the kinds of instructional methods and strategies used, provide examples of professionalism exhibited, and identify areas to improve. The student teacher should be encouraged to focus on knowledge of teaching techniques, subject matter, celebration of success, and goal setting for the future.[12] If the intern has had a positive experience, it is important that he have the cooperating teacher's school and home contact information to add to his professional resume. This will allow prospective employers a contact point if they should have questions about this potential employee. Because many student teachers move at the end of their experience, a permanent address such as the parents' should be shared with the mentor.

CHAPTER SUMMARY

A well-planned student teaching experience depends on short- and long-term planning facilitated by the mentor and university supervisor. Mentors who are good managers of time and demonstrate effective planning skills are best equipped to help student teachers. At the beginning of the student teaching experience, the mentor needs to be directive, making sure expectations and needed information are understood and provided. A sequence for having the student teacher assume teaching and responsibilities need to be developed and shared with both the intern and university supervisor. The progress of the student teacher, as discussed in frequent formative conferences, may result in modifying this plan.

Ideally, an intern will become increasingly reflective and able to evaluate performance throughout the experience. Feedback is crucial to the student teacher's optimal professional growth at all stages of the experience. Continuing to share observations about the intern's performance, interactions, and growth throughout the experience will help make the assignment and future teaching successful.

NOTES

1. Lawrence Lyman, "A Professor Returns to the Classroom in a Professional Development School," *ERIC Resources in Education* (paper presented at the national conference of the Kansas University Professional Development Schools Alliance, Kansas City, Mo., February 2000).

2. Tom Ganser, "The Contribution of Service as a Cooperating Teacher and Mentor Teacher to the Professional Development of Teachers" (paper presented at the annual meeting of the American Educational Research Association, Chicago, March 1997), 1–62.

3. Tara S. Azwell, Harvey C. Foyle, Lawrence Lyman, and Nancy L. Smith, *Constructing Curriculum in Context* (Dubuque, Iowa: Kendall/Hunt, 1999), 12–18.

4. Azwell et al., *Constructing Curriculum in Context*, 543–47.

5. Azwell et al., *Constructing Curriculum in Context*, 549–65.

6. Harvey C. Foyle, Michael A. Morehead, and Lawrence Lyman, *Conferencing with Student Teachers: The Beginning Conference* (New York: Insight Media, 1992), videotape.

7. C. M. Charles, *Building Classroom Discipline from Models to Practice* (New York: Longman, 1989), 27–39.

8. Joseph J. Caruso, "Cooperating Teacher and Student Teacher Phases of Development," *Young Children* 55, no. 1 (January 2000): 75–81.

9. Caruso, "Cooperating Teacher and Student Teacher," 75–81.

10. J. M. Cooper, "Supervision in Teacher Education," *International Encyclopedia of Teaching and Teacher Education* (1995): 593–98.

11. Ken Zeichner and D. P. Liston, "Teaching Student Teachers to Reflect," *Harvard Educational Review* 57 (1987): 23–48.

12. Foyle et al., *Conferencing with Student Teachers*.

CHAPTER 5

Supervising the Student Teacher

Appropriate supervision of the student teacher is essential for positive, professional growth. Quality supervision depends on the ability of mentors to build a positive, professional relationship with the intern, and to plan and organize the student teacher's professional activities efficiently. Effective supervisors have the ability to collect necessary data about the student teacher's performance and reflect on it during formative and summative conferences.[1] Supervisors need to be skillful in reinforcing appropriate behaviors and attitudes while helping the intern clarify decision-making processes. Brainstorming solutions to instructional and behavior problems and remediating areas of weakness or concern are also essential for successful supervision.

TWO MODELS OF SUPERVISION

The model of supervision utilized by mentors impacts the way they interact with student teachers. Although many models of supervision exist, most can be summarized as models of either congruency or discrepancy. Both models can theoretically improve the performance and professional growth, but the congruency model tends to result in more positive attitudes toward the supervision process.[2]

Supervisors who use congruency as a model for supervision seek to identify areas of strength in performance. The supervisor looks for actions that are effective in helping the student learn. When conferring with the student teacher, the supervisor emphasizes the positive aspects of performance and identifies strengths whenever possible.

Supervisors who use a discrepancy model concentrate on areas of weakness in performance. The supervisor looks for actions that are interfering with student learning. When conferencing, the supervisor emphasizes the aspects of the student teacher's performance that are inhibiting positive instruction. The focus of the supervisory conference is on weaknesses and how they can be modified.

When mentors use a congruency model of supervision, conferences are more positive because the student teacher gains confidence from knowing what is being done well. When the student teacher understands that her practices are congruent with effective teaching, she is more likely to use such methods more often in future teaching, both in the present assignment and eventually in her own classroom. Perhaps the most important benefit of responding to supervision in a caring, positive manner is that the interns are more likely to respond similarly to their own students.[3] The congruency model is most helpful throughout the intern's experience and is primarily formative in approach. The discrepancy model is used when interns continue to make mistakes and find it difficult to modify behavior. If a supervisor uses the discrepancy model, she must be aware of its impact on trust and how the intern will communicate in the future. The discrepancy model should be used with caution, but it is a necessary tool that sometimes must be used.

FORMATIVE AND SUMMATIVE CONFERENCES

Supervisors use two basic types of conferences with student teachers. In formative conferences, the intern and supervisor work together to identify effective and ineffective teaching strategies, behaviors, and attitudes. Formative conferences also involve planning and goal setting for the future. This type of conference is ongoing throughout the experience and occurs both formally and informally. Mentors should plan at least one formative conference per week, realizing that there should be numerous interactions that consist of formative discussions each day. Planning and scheduling formative conferences ensure that they take place each week.

Summative conferences are evaluative in nature. Such conferences typically occur at the midpoint and end of the student teaching experience. Additional summative conferences may be necessary if an intern is not meeting the expectations of the supervisors. During the summative conference, supervisors typically share results of previous evaluations of performance and make appropriate suggestions for improvement in the future.

Formative conferences are usually more useful than summative conferences because they provide specific feedback that can be quickly implemented by an intern. These conferences are usually less formal and more loosely structured than summative conferences, which encourages honesty and openness. When held on a regular basis, formative conferences help in omitting surprise and anxiety from the evaluation process. If executed appropriately, data shared in the summative conferences will come from the formative conferences and, therefore, no surprises should occur at the midterm or ending evaluation.

At the beginning of the experience, formative conferences should be supervisor directed.[4] Both the mentor and university supervisor need to ensure that the intern understands the expectations for student teaching and is making a positive adjustment to the classroom. During initial formative conferences, the mentor and supervisor will focus primarily on reinforcing the positive and provide premeditation for any problems or concerns noticed. Addressing and dealing with potential problems early can alleviate serious difficulties that might emerge later. Supervisors should address even minor concerns immediately. Too often, supervisors assume these "little" issues will disappear, only to find out later they are a prelude to more serious concerns. Therefore, the mentor must deal with the little irritants immediately.

As the student teacher gains confidence and experience, the formative conference can become more of a dialogue. Clarifying and brainstorming strategies used by supervisors can encourage the intern to analyze performance and suggest what has gone well and what needs further work. By the end of the student teaching experience, most interns should be encouraged to lead the conference. Analyzing what has taken place in a systematic manner, determining what has gone well, and deciding how to deal with problems are key signals that professional growth has occurred. This process readies the student teacher for his own classroom where such decisions must be made independently.

Keeping a record of the dates and content of formative conferences provides important data, which helps make evaluation easier. A suggested form for a weekly formative conference can be found in table 5.1. Although at least one weekly conference is recommended, mentors may share data any time. Some mentors prefer to share a journal with their student teacher, recording observations and ideas immediately. The intern responds to the mentor's feedback in the journal, facilitating a written dialogue. This process often has an unanticipated outcome—both individuals improve their ability to articulate thoughts and reflections about teaching. This outcome from journal writing usually emerges in deeper and more reflective thinking about teaching.[5]

The records of formative conferences form the basis for the summative evaluation of the student teacher's performance. When accurate records are kept, the supervisor has an invaluable reference to use when completing summative evaluations or writing reference letters for interns. In the event that the student teacher is having difficulty, the formative conference records are important evidence that the student teacher has been provided with frequent feedback about performance. This information and record keeping often proves invaluable when the issue of "due process" is discussed.

University supervisors also find formative conference records helpful. By reading the weekly summary of the discussions between mentor and intern, the university supervisor can compare the triad's assessments of the experience. The supervisor can easily identify areas of concern that were discussed previously. It is also recommended that the formative conference record be shared on a regular basis with the building principal. Because the principal is the instructional leader in the school, it will assist her if parents should call about the class, or in future hiring decisions.

The summative conferences will proceed more professionally when formative conferences have been conducted and weekly records have been kept. The student teacher will tend to be less anxious, since there is already familiarity with issues to be discussed. The final summative conference is more likely to be a celebration of the student teacher's progress and end on a positive note if formative conferences have alleviated previous trouble spots. If there are serious concerns, then the intern has previously been apprised of them through formative conferences.

Table 5.1. Weekly Conference Form and Summative Conference Form Samples

These conference and summative evaluation forms are from the elementary professional development schools, Emporia State University. They are printed on self-duplicating paper with copies distributed as noted. The weekly conference form is usually completed by the student teacher after conferencing with the mentor teacher to reduce mentor teacher paperwork.

Weekly Conference Form

Student Teacher _____   Mentor _____

Week of _____

Conference Agenda:

Target Activities for Next Week:

_____

Student Teacher Signature   Mentor Teacher Signature

_____   _____

Date:

Copies to: student teacher, mentor teacher, principal, university supervisor

---

Evaluation Conference Summary

(Circle appropriate one):   End of first five weeks   End of second five weeks

Student Teacher _____

School Assignment _____ Grade Level _____

Mentor Teacher _____

Strengths Observed

Areas to Work On

Plan for the Next Five Weeks

REINFORCING

One of the most important things a supervisor can do during the supervision process is reinforce desirable instructional behaviors. Reinforcement has numerous important benefits for the student teacher. When reinforcement is genuine and accurate, the intern feels that the supervisor is competent, cares about her success, and feedback is worthwhile. Because the student teacher realizes that the supervisor is interested in his success, trust is enhanced.

When reinforcement is used effectively, an intern is able to make teaching behaviors, which may have been intuitively used, part of a conscious decision-making process in future planning and instruction. Student teachers are more likely to seek help from mentors and supervisors who reinforce effective behaviors than from those who utilized the discrepancy model. The most important benefit of appropriate reinforcement may be that the student teacher is more likely to use the reinforced instructional behaviors, resulting in improved learning and behavior in the classroom.

Effective reinforcement of instructional behaviors results from focus, timeliness, straightforwardness, and a positive tone. Focus results from limiting the number of reinforced behaviors after a single observation. It is more productive to focus on one or two specific behaviors that can be productively used in future lessons. When a supervisor attempts to introduce too many issues, two things can occur. First, the intern can become overwhelmed and, therefore, not able to respond to any recommendations. Second, an intern might begin feeling a serious level of inadequacy and lose confidence that may never be regained.

The value of reinforcement is lessened when too much time passes between the behavior and the reinforcement. Some strategies for reinforcing behavior in a timely manner are a written note or a brief, informal conference with the intern where positive behavior is mentioned. This can be done between classes, during transition time, or during a class break. When reinforcing, the supervisor needs to be straightforward. This means that the supervisor is genuinely reinforcing an appropriate behavior, not using reinforcement as a lead-in to unpleasant information or feedback. This last technique, though sometimes used, creates a level of mistrust and can negatively impact the mentor-intern relationship.

One problem of positive reinforcement is that some student teachers are not comfortable discussing what they do well. An intern may devalue the reinforcement by commenting that the behavior wasn't important, wasn't done satisfactorily, or did not take much effort. When reinforcement takes place often, and supervisors positively confront attempts to devalue efforts, interns will more likely accept reinforcement as a way to recognize quality teaching and enhance future performance.

For reinforcement to be effective in improving student achievement and attitudes in the classroom, teaching behaviors discussed must have a real effect on students in the classroom. Effective instructional behaviors that positively affect student learning can be grouped into five categories; analyzing, prescribing, determining strategies, creating instructional design, and performing assessments. Observable examples of each of these categories can be found in the appendix.

Analyzing behaviors involves the manner in which the student teacher sets goals and objectives for learning. Appropriate diagnosis of diverse student needs is evidence of effective instructional analysis. Analysis also involves making sure that appropriate state and local competencies are being addressed and met.

Prescribing effective ways to organize learning for students requires numerous decisions. When prescribing instructional activities to meet the needs of learners, effective interns will utilize student groupings that bring together students with varying academic abilities. Learning activities should be clearly focused on the instructional objective for a given lesson and the objectives should be clearly understood by students. Prescribing decisions also include ways to facilitate higher-level student thinking, problem solving during instruction, and creative thinking.

Determining appropriate instructional strategies is another category of decision making. Effective student teachers accommodate multiple intelligence levels and make adaptations for the needs of learners. Strategies are selected that help students understand and remember lessons while motivating students to become actively engaged in the learning process. This category also includes management decisions made by the teacher to keep students positively and productively involved.

Effective lesson design includes focusing students on learning and providing an appropriate review of what has been learned previously.

Instructional input and modeling should be clear and focused. The teacher checks for understanding during the lesson and guided practice activities. Closure is provided for each instructional sequence, and appropriate independent practice is assigned.

Assessment decisions take place before, during, and after instruction. Before teaching, the intern needs to determine how the students will demonstrate that they have achieved learning objectives. During instruction, checking for understanding provides information that helps adjust the pace and content of instruction as needed. After instruction, assessment provides evidence of student learning and information on which to base further instruction. How interns use assessment to evaluate their teaching will offer excellent insight for the mentor. If students do not perform well on a given assessment, the intern must reflect on each element of the instructional process to determine the reason for lack of success.

If an intern is concerned about student performance and leading a discussion on how to rectify the problem, she is asking the right questions. However, if an intern is blaming students, parents, or previous teachers, this type of discussion should alert a supervisor of potential problems. If an intern demonstrates this behavior, the supervisors should meet immediately to determine appropriate actions. An intern who is reflecting on student performance from a problem-solving perspective is more likely to be a successful teacher and better meet the needs of students.

The above-described instructional behaviors can assist in guiding the supervision of the instructional process. These five instructional behaviors, if implemented effectively, can positively impact student learning. As a mentor monitors these five behaviors, student learning should be enhanced and the intern's teaching improved.

When reinforcing appropriate teaching behaviors, the mentor or university supervisor should do four things: identify, label, connect, and extend. First, the supervisor should identify the productive behavior that has been observed. This behavior should be one that has positively impacted student learning. Next, the supervisor should label the behavior by giving it a name that the student teacher will recognize in later conferences. This labeling gives both parties a contextual reference for future discussions. Since many different terms for instructional behaviors exist, the student teacher needs to become familiar with what the supervisor is labeling as "motivation" or "guided practice."

The third factor in effective reinforcement is connecting the behavior to student learning. The supervisor should tell how the behavior helped students to understand a concept or idea or how interest and motivation were facilitated. Finally, the supervisor should, when appropriate, extend the behavior to other teaching situations by suggesting how this teaching behavior could be appropriately used in other situations. To assist the professional growth of an intern, the supervisor could ask the student teacher to offer suggestions of where and how this behavior could be used in the other classroom experiences. Examples of clarification questions can assist in the process.

CLARIFICATION

Clarification is the appropriate use of questioning to gain understanding and facilitate student teacher participation in formative and summative conferences. Benefits of clarification include improved dialog between interns and supervisors, improved understanding of decision making processes, more accurate analysis of performance, and encouragement for self-analysis by the student teacher.[6]

As the intern becomes more skilled and gains confidence, it is appropriate to involve him more in the supervisory conference. Clarification helps accomplish this by asking participants to analyze their teaching behavior. When using clarification, it is important that the supervisor listen carefully and ask follow-up questions to promote understanding. Clarification questions must seek information, not make statements or imply judgments. For example, asking if a student teacher was aware that four students in the back of the room were off task during a lesson is not necessarily a question but rather a statement of concern about management skills. Some appropriate clarification questions can be found in table 5.2.

Helping a supervisor gain understanding about a lesson from a student teacher's perspective is an important use of clarification questions. Asking how an intern decided students were ready for the lesson, for example, assists a supervisor's understanding of how decisions about

Table 5.2.   Examples of Clarification Questions

1. How did you feel about the lesson you taught?
2. What things turned out well?
3. What strategies could you use when you teach again tomorrow?
4. If you were going to teach this lesson again, would you do anything differently?
5. What strategies did you use to ensure that the students understood what you were teaching?
6. How did you keep students on task during the lesson?
7. Which management strategy worked the best for you during this lesson?
8. How did you keep students engaged in the instruction?
9. How did you feel about the new strategy you tried during this lesson?
10. What did you learn from teaching this lesson?

content and organization of instruction were determined. Asking about selected instructional strategies for a particular lesson lets a supervisor know how decisions are made about content and the use of teaching methods. Assessment decisions can be better understood by asking how the intern knew students understood what was being taught or why a decision was made on a particular assessment strategy for a given instructional sequence.

Clarification questions can also be used to check the intern's perceptions about students and how they reacted to a lesson. Asking for an analysis of class motivation or of an individual student's attentiveness helps the teacher think about what was observed while teaching. Inquiring about positive aspects of the lesson allows the supervisor to know how the student teacher is analyzing his or her own teaching.

Clarification strategies can help establish a positive tone during present and future conferences. At the beginning of a conference, for example, a supervisor should ask what aspects of a lesson pleased the student teacher. A positive statement may precede a question designed to set a positive tone. One example is, "I noticed the students were really involved in the lesson this morning. How did you get them so interested?" This question lets the intern know the supervisor noticed positive things about a lesson and encourages sharing.

The university supervisor is less involved with the day-to-day instructional process in the classroom than the cooperating teacher. During university supervisor visits, clarification helps a supervisor understand what went on in class prior to the supervisor's visit and how the student teacher intends to continue. Afterwards, if the supervisor feels students have not understood a concept well, it may be more appropriate to clarify than give advice. If the response to a clarification question indicates an intern was aware of the problem and has planned an appropriate strategy for reteaching the next day, then a supervisor can reinforce this decision. By using clarification as depicted above, the student teacher will be more actively involved in the supervision process and able to mature professionally.

University supervisors may find it helpful to ask if the lessons observed during the visit were typical for that group of students. Special circumstances of which the supervisor was unaware may have affected the students' behaviors and attitudes during the lesson. When the intern clarifies, for example, that students were uninterested in the fractions lesson because the class hamster had escaped and they were still on "hamster watch," the supervisor is saved from attempting to remediate when it may not be necessary.

University supervisors sometimes visit when student teachers and their students are not at their best. When the supervisor observes or learns through clarification that the observation is not typical of what normally goes on in the classroom, the university supervisor should schedule another visit soon to observe a more representative example of teaching. This helps assure an intern that the supervisor is committed to being helpful and supportive.

During each visit, the university representative should visit with the cooperating teacher to evaluate a variety of topics. Using clarifying questions with the mentor will assist in determining if the mentor's and intern's perceptions and reflections are similar. When perceptions are similar, usually a positive experience is taking place. If the supervisor receives mixed messages and determines that perceptions by the mentor and intern are different, it will be necessary to have a three-way conference to determine the degree of discrepancy.

BRAINSTORMING

In order to meet the needs of their many diverse students, interns need to become skilled problem solvers. The ability to respond to students in new and different ways is one of the hallmarks of teacher effectiveness.

Trying new strategies requires the encouragement of both supervisors. Unfortunately, supervisors often provide answers and solutions to student problems rather than encourage the student teacher to use creative problem-solving strategies.[7]

Brainstorming provides an opportunity for the intern and supervisor to think of alternative strategies for meeting student needs in the classroom. When an intern has been successful with students, brainstorming can be used to determine ways to build on the successful experience. Brainstorming can also be used to design alternative approaches for instruction, management, or assessment when a problem or concern has developed. Planning for future instruction is also an area in which brainstorming may be helpful. If possible, it would be appropriate to involve other teachers or interns in this process. The opportunity to share and create with peers can be an excellent professional development activity.

Brainstorming usually focuses on one of three primary goals: fluency, originality, or flexibility. Fluency involves thinking of as many ideas as possible. Often, student teachers develop a single idea or strategy rather than exploring many. Some of the most creative ideas can come after many different ideas have been introduced, analyzed, and discussed.

Originality involves thinking of strategies that are new to the individual. For example, a student teacher may decide to try expanding on a strategy that has been used previously with success. The intern may also be willing to try an approach suggested in a methods class. Originality may also involve a shift of paradigms, with new priorities becoming the focus of efforts.

Flexibility is perhaps the most demanding of the three brainstorming goals. Flexibility requires that the student teacher shift from old patterns of thinking and reflect in ways that may require a new thought process. Flexibility may be particularly uncomfortable since old habits of thinking and approaching problem solving may be deeply ingrained. To utilize brainstorming, the mentor or university supervisor needs to be sure sufficient time is provided. Identifying original ideas to solve challenging problems involving students is not easy, and solutions cannot be determined without a commitment of time and energy.

As with many aspects of the supervision process, the degree of trust between supervisor and student teacher influences a willingness to be creative and consider ideas that may seem risky. When trust is present, the intern feels more comfortable in suggesting ideas that may, without explanation, seem unproductive or even silly. In classrooms, student teachers will need to think creatively to solve the inevitable problems that occur. Letting the intern participate in developing possible solutions to problems prepares her to accept this challenge.

Encouraging the student teacher to become an active participant in brainstorming and problem solving provides an opportunity for shared responsibility between all parties in the triad. If a supervisor suggests a solution to a problem, the student teacher may be less committed to implementing it and blame the supervisor if success is not achieved.

Brainstorming requires that a supervisor help the intern become comfortable with uncertainty. There is hardly a single correct answer for any given classroom challenge, and what has worked in one situation may now work in another. Student teachers need to understand that when a solution is unsuccessful, it does not mean failure but rather indicates a willingness to try a variety of strategies and demonstrates flexibility. All ideas are valuable when brainstorming, and they should be considered as future options for instruction or solving particular problems.

Divergent questions are often the most successful technique used when brainstorming to generate a variety of options. Divergent questions are open ended. The supervisor should not attempt to steer the student teacher toward a particular answer or idea by asking the questions. Divergent questions can help participants think about information already known or experienced and apply that information to occurring problems. Supervisors may also use divergent questions to help an intern reflect on different strategies while solving problems in the classroom. In the event the student teacher is unable to think of possible alternatives, the supervisor should have several workable strategies in mind to suggest.

Convergent questions, which have only one correct answer, are not usually helpful when brainstorming and usually limit or end discussion of new ideas. Similarly, evaluative questions, which require value judgments and can usually be answered with yes or no, also hinder the brainstorming process. It is sometimes helpful for the supervisor to use the strategy of "hitchhiking" when brainstorming with an intern. Hitchhiking occurs when the supervisor adds information, ideas, or suggestions to the student teacher's responses. Hitchhiking can produce a helpful professional dialog between the supervisor and student teacher.

REMEDIATION

It is sometimes necessary to use part of a conference for remediation. Remediation is the process of correcting inappropriate decisions or actions and redirecting the student teacher to more appropriate strategies. Remediation does not need to be threatening and is a useful part of the learning process.

At the beginning of the experience, the mentor will likely use remediation to help the student teacher understand the mentor's expectations. A simple correction early can avoid problems and behaviors that might irritate the mentor later in the assignment. Most teachers, when establishing a classroom climate at the beginning of a new year, respond quickly to students whose behaviors do not meet their expectations. This quick response to behaviors exhibited by an intern is also necessary and can alleviate potential communication problems in the future. For example, if an intern is not turning in paperwork in a timely manner or is arriving later, it is essential to remediate these behaviors early.

Remediation is also needed when actions by the student teacher violate appropriate teaching practices. Supervisors need to make sure interns understand the behavior or strategy that is unacceptable and why. The cooperating teacher also needs to suggest a specific alternative that the student teacher will be expected to utilize. For example, sometimes beginning teachers respond to only a handful of students such as the brightest or those in need of more attention because of behavior issues. Whatever the cause, a mentor must point this out and offer positive alternatives for the intern to implement.

Remediation is most effective when the supervisor follows up with positive reinforcement as the concern is remedied or the alternative successfully employed. Unfortunately, not all problems with student teachers are simple ones. Continued difficulty with the same areas or serious areas of concern may require more intense remediation. This topic is covered in detail in chapter 6.

Whether the remediation is something as simple as turning in paperwork on time, or as significant as giving misinformation when teaching, all issues should be dealt with as soon as possible. Often, cooperating teachers hope that a particular problem will dissipate with time, but this hardly ever happens. Most of the time, the problem persists and the mentor becomes frustrated, which builds over time. By not dealing with the concern early, an intern is less likely to see the significance once addressed. Compounded with the frustration of a mentor, the problem is likely to escalate and become more significant than is necessary. This is why early remediation is so important and essential.

USING TECHNOLOGY TO PROVIDE FEEDBACK TO STUDENT TEACHERS

The availability of electronic mail can allow the university supervisor to communicate more often with the student teacher and increase the amount of feedback. The university supervisor should require that the student teacher communicate by e-mail at least once a week. This communication does not need to be lengthy, but should include a brief reflection on what has been accomplished during the week and what is planned for the next one. Lesson plans can also be sent to the university supervisor via e-mail. The supervisor can analyze the lesson plans and return comments and suggestions promptly without visiting the school. If a journal is required, sharing reflections can keep the university supervisor informed. Technology allows this form of communication to occur and enhances the experience.[8]

CHAPTER SUMMARY

Effective supervision helps achieve the maximum benefit from the student teaching experience. Mentors and university supervisors who model congruency in their interactions with student teachers are usually more successful and influential. Frequent formative conferences help promote professional growth and expertise, and when appropriately used, summative evaluation is easier and less stressful for all involved.

Supervisors need to be able to reinforce appropriate teaching behaviors and attitudes exhibited by the intern. As the student teacher gains skill, clarification and brainstorming may be used to facilitate more active involvement and participation by the student teacher in conferences. Remediation of inappropriate decisions and behaviors is most successful when concerns are identified early by the supervisor and followed up by positive reinforcement.

NOTES

1. Lawrence Lyman, Alfred P. Wilson, C. Kent Garhart, Max O. Heim, and Wynona O. Winn, *Clinical Instruction and Supervision for Accountability* (Dubuque, Iowa: Kendall/Hunt, 1987), 100–113.

2. Lawrence Lyman, Michael A. Morehead, and Harvey C. Foyle, "Building Teacher Trust in Supervision and Evaluation," *Illinois School Research and Development* 25, no. 2 (Winter 1989): 55–59.

3. Lawrence Lyman and Harvey C. Foyle, *Cooperative Grouping for Interactive Learning: Students, Teachers, and Administrators* (Washington, D.C.: National Education Association, 1990), 25.

4. Jacquelyn W. Jensen, "Supervision from Six Theoretical Frameworks" (paper presented at the annual meeting of the American Educational Research Association, San Diego, April 1998), 1–34.

5. Dian Yendol Silva, "Triad Journaling as a Tool for Reconceptualizing Supervision in the Professional Development School" (paper presented at the annual meeting of the American Educational Research Association, New Orleans, April 2000), 1–17.

6. Lawrence Lyman and Harvey C. Foyle, "Creative Supervisory Conferences: New Wine in Old Skins?" *Florida ASCD Journal* 6 (Fall 1989): 45–46.

7. Lyman and Foyle, "Creative Supervisory Conferences: New Wine in Old Skins?" 45–47.

8. Silva, "Triad Journaling as a Tool for Reconceptualizing Supervision," 1–17.

CHAPTER 6

Helping Student Teachers Succeed in Diverse Classrooms

Today's student teachers will work in schools that are becoming increasingly diversified. Inclusion of more special-needs students in regular classrooms challenges all educators to design lessons that are appropriate for a wide range of learning abilities and styles.[1] Student teachers are also challenged to provide equitable learning opportunities for students so that all can be successful, regardless of socioeconomic status, language, ethnicity, gender, or ability.[2] Mentor teachers and university supervisors need to provide instructional assistance and feedback to interns so that they can be successful in today's educationally diverse settings.

GETTING TO KNOW STUDENTS

If interns are to meet the needs of all students, the first step is becoming acquainted with the diversity in the classroom and learning about students' personalities, interests, and backgrounds. One strategy might be to conduct structured interviews with students. This activity, with individual students or small groups of students, helps the intern build trust and positive relationships with children early in the experience. The mentor or university supervisor may want to provide a list of interview questions to be used in this exercise and encourage the use of questions provided while conducting the interviews. Possible interview questions can be found in table 2.2. The intern should make notes of useful information about each student and will sometimes discover information about students that the mentor is unaware of. Sharing the results of these interviews during formative conferences is suggested.

As discussed in chapter 4, guided observation of the class can help an intern become acquainted with the students and provide an opportunity to check the accuracy of his perceptions about students. If inaccuracies or biases are evident, the mentor can assist the student teacher in developing a more accurate and tolerant view of students.

In the first days of the experience, the mentor and intern should discuss the makeup of the class. Gender, religious groups, and ethnic demographics must be reviewed together. Student teachers today are more culturally sensitive and aware than they were ten years ago, but even with the emphasis on multicultural themes increasing in teacher education programs, student teachers may not be aware of situations that are particular to the region, district, or school. Mentors must warn interns about "taboos" that exist because of cultural or even legal decisions they may have to make. For example, in science, performing experiments with certain animals may not be acceptable. In art, depicting certain individuals or animals in a particular manner may not be appropriate in the area or district. Even the celebration of the Christmas holiday in many areas is limited to very specific activities. Making student teachers aware of these issues early will keep them from making serious mistakes that would offend some in the community and in the class.

Interns who participate in the beginning of the school year have opportunities to observe how the teacher uses group-building activities to create a community in the classroom. These activities provide opportunities for all students to develop an appreciation for individual differences and encourage students to view each other and the teacher as members of the classroom community. Such activities are necessary at the beginning of the school year and throughout the year in order to sustain successful collaboration among students.[3] An example of a group-building activity can be found in table 6.1.

When the intern observes students interacting during group-building activities, important information about interpersonal skills of students, academic strengths and weaknesses, and cliques that may try to dominate activities can be determined. This information can be valuable to the intern while planning to meet the needs of all students, especially if cooperative learning groups are used.

Table 6.1.   Sample Group-Building Activity

This group-building activity would be suitable for students in a secondary social studies class.

People Search

Find someone to sign each box. You need to find a different person to sign each box.

	Signature		*Signature*
Find someone who can tell you the first sentence of the Gettysburg Address.		Find someone who can tell you what two words were added to the Pledge of Allegiance during the 1950s.	
Find someone who can tell you the address of the White House on Pennsylvania Avenue.		Find someone who can tell you the approximate population of the world.	
Find someone who can whistle or hum a patriotic song.		Find someone who can play a musical instrument.	
Find someone who can tell you whose picture is on the $5 bill.		Find someone who took pictures of a trip they took last summer.	
Find someone who likes to dance.		Find someone who played on a high school or college sports team.	
Find someone who can name the vice president of the United States.		Find someone who worked on a committee in the past year where the members worked well together.	
Find someone who has written a letter to a newspaper.		Find someone who has kept a diary or journal.	
Find someone who can name an extinct animal.		Find someone who can tell you when the next full moon will occur.	

Source: Lawrence Lyman and Harvey C. Foyle, "Lessons Learned from a Multiculturally, Economically Diverse Classroom Setting" (paper presented at the 79th annual conference, National Council for the Social Studies, Orlando, Fla., November 20, 1999).

PROMOTING EQUITABLE TEACHING PRACTICES

Providing students with equitable opportunities for involvement and success should be a goal of every teacher. Supervisors can provide valuable feedback to enhance the student teachers' awareness of practices they use that encourage or discourage student involvement and success.

If students are to be involved and successful while the intern is working with them, they must be accorded opportunities for participation and given positive feedback about their accomplishments. As the student teacher begins to reach whole-group lessons, the mentor and supervisor should observe instructional sequences and record data about interactions with students. Initially, the mentor and university supervisor will want to observe the intern's interaction patterns with students. Data can be gathered by using a copy of the class seating chart. During a class discussion, for example, a mark can be made on the seating chart as students are called upon. This coding of observational data can be shared with the student teacher during formative conferences to encourage the student teacher to provide opportunities for involvement and success for all students.

While moving about the classroom, a mark on the seating chart can be made when the intern stops to help or interact with a student. Interactions with students at the beginning of class, during passing periods, and at the end of class can also be recorded. The goal of these observations is to provide the intern with information about which students are receiving attention and which students are not. During the formative conference, this information can be shared to help identify students who are not involved and better reflect on the intern's interactions with students.

Students also need equitable opportunities to experience success in the classroom. A seating chart can again be used to record interactions between the intern and students. When noting successful opportunities, the mentor or university supervisor records a "+" on the seating chart when a student answers a question correctly or receives feedback that is positive. If a student is unsuccessful or negative feedback is given, the "-" symbol can be used. If the student is initially unsuccessful, but a prompt from the teacher results in a successful response from the student, the "+" symbol would follow the "-" symbol. This indicates the intern helped the student succeed with teacher assistance. This may seem a bit confusing, but after a couple of class observations, the coding process will become easy.

As the student teacher begins taking over more of the instruction in the classroom, the mentor or supervisor can provide additional feedback about the kinds of response opportunities being offered to students. While observing a lesson in which the student teacher is using questioning during a class discussion, the cooperating teacher or university supervisor can make a list of the questions asked and to whom.

During formative conferences, the mentor or supervisor helps the intern analyze questions asked during the lesson. Questions that promote recall or lower-level cognitive responses are identified. Questions that encourage higher-level cognition, problem solving, or creativity are also noted. The mentor or university supervisor then helps the intern analyze which students were asked higher-level questions. The goal for the student teacher is to be aware that all students need opportunities for critical and creative thinking. As the student teacher matures professionally, the mentor may request that the intern do the same coding of observational data while the mentor teaches. This guided observation will enhance dialogue and allow the mentor to observe the depth of understanding about teaching by the intern.

As the intern begins to check students' work, the mentor should review work that has been corrected. The first concern is to ensure that the student teacher has been accurate in his assessment of student work. Important in this process is consideration for varying student academic abilities, strengths, and limitations. The mentor should encourage the student teacher to notice something positive about the work of each student.[4] As the mentor looks though corrected work, she should note when positive comments have been made. This practice should be encouraged and interns should make positive comments on as many papers as possible when assessing students' work. This strategy enables students to recognize their own success and encourages them to use similar strategies in future assignments. Assessment strategies must be multiple in nature and include a variety of techniques. It is no longer acceptable to utilize only paper-and-pencil forms of assessment. Most student teachers have been introduced to multiple assessment techniques during their preservice program. Cooperating teachers must give them the opportunity to use a variety of assessment strategies.

PLANNING FOR DIVERSITY

As the intern plans for instruction, the mentor will typically be involved in making sure instructional plans are appropriate for the needs, interests, and developmental levels of a diverse student population. To meet the needs of a wide range of learners, student teachers need to adapt and modify instructional outcomes. Adapting instructional tasks for differing abilities is necessary so all students can feel successful and challenged by the curriculum. When students are asked to perform too difficult or easy tasks, frustration and management problems can result.[5]

Student teachers should be encouraged to appropriately assign lessons for the needs of students by including adaptations as part of their planning and implementation. For example, students who are highly motivated may be given modified questions and asked to assist another when finished; some may need more time, increased support, or modified instruction to be successful. Student teachers may also need to adapt the difficulty level of the learning task for the student or vary the way in which the student demonstrates success.[6] This can be accomplished by the way in which students are assessed. Table 6.2 offers a list of assessment strategies.

USING A VARIETY OF TEACHING STRATEGIES

In order to meet the needs of diverse students, interns must be required to use a variety of instructional practices. No one way of teaching can be expected to work for all students.[7] A common limitation at the secondary level is the lack of modeling of, and expected use of, numerous instructional strategies.

Howard Gardner has identified eight different intelligence areas that can be identified in students who are present in today's schools.[8] As beginners in the classroom, however, many student teachers limit their

Table 6.2. Ways to Assess Student Performance

 1. Teacher observations
 2. Student verbal response
 3. Portfolios
 4. Cooperative activities
 5. Written assignments
 6. Testing
 7. Hands-on activities
 8. Oral analysis of topic
 9. Written analysis of topic
10. Art activities related to topic
11. Physical representation developed by student
12. Role-playing

teaching to one or two intelligence areas, often concentrating on the verbal and mathematical forms.

Mentors can assist by identifying strategies that meet diverse student needs by using a variety of activities designed to appeal to different intelligence areas. For instruction to be successful with all students, it must be designed to link to the learning strengths and intelligence areas of students.[9]

Interns often utilize paper-and-pencil tasks that require the use of verbal intelligence. It is also important for interns to provide opportunities for students to communicate with others in the classroom, thereby using and improving language skills. Since the primary purpose of acquiring language skills is to communicate with others effectively, students need opportunities to communicate with each other, learn about each other, resolve differences, and solve learning problems cooperatively.[10]

The overuse of written activities may place the second language leaners at a disadvantage in the classroom. Interns must be encouraged to support the learning of second language learners through activities that allow them to practice language skills in nonthreatening and authentic ways. Puppet shows, role-playing, and student-produced news shows are just a few ways to involve students who are acquiring new language skills. These examples of nonthreatening strategies will enhance the learning atmosphere of a classroom for all students.[11]

Logical intelligence can be useful in helping students become critical and creative thinkers. Interns should plan activities that encourage students to use problem-solving skills and metacognition as critical thinkers.[12] Interns also need to encourage students to approach learning tasks creatively. Activities that move beyond basic skills and factual information can encourage students to generate ideas they might not think of otherwise.[13]

Mentors should encourage the use of movement activities that complement the body-kinesthetic intelligence to assist in meeting diverse learners' needs. In all grades, but especially in the early elementary experience, students have a particular need for learning activities that incorporate movement. These activities can be integrated with other intelligence areas to involve students in developmentally appropriate learning experiences.[14]

Mentors should help the interns monitor students' nonverbal cues to determine when a break is needed. At the elementary level, a short warm-up movement activity at the beginning of the day may help students be more alert and participate. At the secondary level, a teacher can use transition times or modify seating during a class period to enhance active participation. Student teachers can get additional ideas for incorporating appropriate body-kinesthetic activities from the physical education teacher or others in the school who use physical learning activities in their curriculum.

Integrating music in lessons should be encouraged and may be used to relax students when entering the class or as background music for study. Some teachers may find a rhythmic clapping pattern a useful strategy for gaining student attention. Harry Wong describes several activities that utilize rhythm or pattering.[15] Both musical and physical activities can enhance the learning opportunities for all students and increase the instructional techniques available to the intern. Using music or physical activities that are part of other cultures validates the culture and demonstrates a teacher's respect for it.

Pictures, diagrams, charts, and graphic organizers complement the visual intelligence area of students. The mentor and university supervisor should observe the use of visual materials as lessons are presented and encourage utilizing these mechanisms on a regular basis. Pictures from students' cultures will enhance the feeling of belonging and create an atmosphere where students can relate to the content.

Interns should also be alert to the physical appearance of the classroom. Is student work on display? If so, does the work represent all students in the class? To increase student interest and involvement, interns can take snapshots of students as they are engaged in learning activities and display them. Art teachers can provide interns with other ideas for integrating visual activities into their teaching. Allowing time to visit other classes and noting the things teachers display in their rooms should be included as part of the intern's experience. Displaying a student's work indicates that the teacher respects the diversity of the students and values them as individuals.

Culture

Interpersonal intelligence refers to the ability to communicate effectively with a variety of cultures. Student teachers should be encouraged to incorporate cooperative learning activities into lessons to promote involvement and build interpersonal skills for all students. Group-building activities can provide opportunities for diverse students to cooperate and build a classroom community. For example, the use of class meetings can encourage group communication and problem solving when difficulties arise in the classroom. When conducting these meetings, the intern should monitor student interaction and make sure ethnically diverse students have an opportunity for input. Counselors can provide strategies for helping manage student conflict, teaching social skills, enhancing interpersonal skills, and balancing gender interactions.

Interns should provide ethnically diverse students opportunities to develop self-awareness and confidence. De-emphasizing the importance of external evaluation tools and encouraging students to reflect on their own progress and effort should also be a part of the experience. During a time of accountability and standardized testing, some students feel they are inadequate and a failure because of their test scores. This is especially true for many second language learners and those from lower socioeconomic situations. It is essential that interns understand the impact these scores can have on students and their perception of future expectations and success. Educators should communicate that standardized test scores are just one small piece of information about a student and are not indicative of overall intelligence or potential for success.

Reflection journals provide all students with an opportunity to personalize learning and think about how learning is important. Portfolios maintained by students provide documentation of learning and allow educators to assess student performance in multiple ways. Journals and portfolios are important elements in classrooms that meet the needs of diverse learners. These materials can also be learning tools for the intern. Personal reflection is important and can provide direction for the intern's professional growth.

Language

The academic discipline's language and the language ability of the student have a profound influence on the classroom environment. Many children enter the classroom not speaking English and not understanding the culture of the school. Beginning teachers must be made aware of and develop instructional strategies that can ensure these students' success in school. Language of the learner and academic discipline significantly impact potential success. This is true for all students, but is even more critical for those whose first language is not English and especially for those where English is not spoken in the home. Student teachers need to know about the language background and level of English proficiency of their students.

Beginning educators usually are not aware that the "academic languages" used in the classroom may not be familiar to all students, and especially challenging for those with limited English proficiency. Making student teachers aware that they must clearly define academic terms is not enough. Interns must be able to define, describe, model, and make available physical representations of the concepts. Without these skills, beginning teachers will not be able to assist all students in their future classrooms.

Secondary teachers must be particularly aware of these issues. Although "academic language" is very familiar to them, it will often be alien to students in their classes. One of the biggest pitfalls that can impact a student teacher's success is the assumption of prior knowledge or understanding by students. Even if the students were previously instructed about a concept or topic, time has passed or a different context for delivery was used and, therefore, students may seem confused or lost. Second language learners can especially fall prey to the "academic language" issue and must be nurtured in such a way as to understand the context of usage.

Bias

Bias takes on many forms and occurs between students, between teacher and students, and appears in the academic setting through textbooks, standardized tests, and in class instruction. Student teachers today have been made aware of multicultural issues and biases that emerge in obvious and subtle ways. Most interns today are much more cognizant of these issues than were their mentors when they student taught.

Assisting the intern in identifying bias in books, curriculum, and even in instruction is essential to their future success. Bias takes on many shapes and often goes unnoticed by the untrained observer. As the relationship between mentor and intern matures and trust is secured, the mentor and intern should attempt to identify bias in their teaching.

Most teachers feel they are free of bias and often express it by saying, "I treat all students equally" or "I do not see color in my classroom." Those statements will be a major warning to an intern or visiting supervisor who is well versed in multicultural themes. Excellent teachers and truly unbiased educators will treat children differently. What they really do is respect the child's culture and language and value each student's background. Excellent teachers also realize that students have different abilities and meet those needs by varying instruction, assignments, and assessment strategies.

Finally if an intern today hears the cooperating teacher say, "Well, you know how those people are" and making a generalization about an ethnic group, there will be an immediate loss of respect and trust. If a teacher has this type of perception or attitude about others, he should not be a cooperating teacher.

Assessment

Varying assessment techniques is part of any excellent teacher's approach in the classroom. Interns must be aware of numerous techniques and be able to integrate those within the instructional process. In order to meet the learning styles or cultural needs of students, a teacher must vary how learning is assessed. Cooperating teachers should model how they assess student learning and allow the intern to visit other teachers who approach assessment differently. Establishing a successful classroom requires the use of multiple forms of assessment and allows students with different language skills the opportunity to succeed. Paper-and-pencil assessment should be a part of any plan but must not be the sole manner in which a teacher assesses student learning.

Finally, like so many other issues related to teaching, the intern and supervisors must discuss at length cultural, language, bias, and assessment issues throughout the experience. Ignoring these will not give an intern a true opportunity for future success. Zimpher and Ashburn point out the importance of discussing cultural issues and the challenges teachers face each day.[16] These discussions should be ongoing and should be conducted in both written and oral forms. As the intern progresses through the experience, the focus will move from "What should I be doing?" to "What do the students need?" Once this transition takes place, the intern has taken a major step toward becoming a teacher.

CREATING MEANING

Mentors and university supervisors should encourage student teachers to find ways to make learning meaningful for all students. As we know, relating the content of lessons to the needs, interests, and cultures of students can increase involvement and reduce management problems. Authentic learning tasks encourage student involvement and help make learning meaningful. Student teachers should develop learning around tasks that are related to real-life experiences and situations that reflect and value the cultures represented in the class.

Zeichner describes the need for high expectations for all students and the use of scaffolding that relates home and cultural experiences to school. Zeichner points out that school customs and expectations must be addressed and that students from diverse backgrounds need to be cognizant of these in order to succeed. Therefore, part of an intern's experience must include the opportunity to instruct students in the customs of schooling. Additionally, high expectations and supporting academic experiences with cultural foundations of the student also enhance opportunities for success. Cooperating teachers must ensure that interns approach all students with these expectations.[17]

Management

Classroom management in diverse settings is the key to success for the student teacher. Supervisors need to ensure discipline strategies utilized by interns are appropriate for student developmental levels and that students are not embarrassed or humiliated. Understanding how students from different cultures react to teacher supervision is important information for an intern. Treating students with respect, being nonthreatening, and giving students options will increase an intern's opportunity for success with all students. It is especially important to understand how respect is demonstrated in certain cultures. For example, many teachers expect a student to look at them when discussing a discipline situation, but in some cultures, that is a sign of disrespect. Alerting an intern to this type of cultural behavior will assist the intern when interacting with students.

Additionally, if the intern follows the procedures and regulations of the mentor, the transition will be smoother when assuming full responsibility for the classroom. If the intern attempts to stray from already established rules and procedures, a disconnect will occur with students and the transition will be very difficult. As the intern assumes increased responsibility for teaching in the classroom, the mentor should monitor management of the classroom to ensure that positive reinforcement is being given to all students. When students' behaviors are addressed, the mentor needs to ensure that this is implemented without favoritism and in a nonthreatening manner. Nonthreatening behaviors demonstrated by the intern could include, but are not limited to, speaking in a softer voice, slowing pace of speech, tone of voice, awareness of nonverbal and facial cues, and meeting privately with the student.

The cooperating teacher also needs to be certain that the intern is aware of situations in the classroom in which students may feel threatened. Since bullying and harassment are inappropriate behaviors, the mentor needs to make sure the intern acts proactively to deal with these issues. Inappropriate use of sarcasm, put-downs, or threats by the student teacher should be noted and stopped immediately. Because of the diversity of the student population, these behaviors are not appropriate for the classroom and may be interpreted as offensive to the student. Teachers who utilize these behaviors have a negative effect on students with often serious, unknown consequences. If this behavior is not corrected immediately, the entire experience is in jeopardy.

The Mentor Teacher as Model

The mentor is the professional model with whom the student teacher will have the most contact and the most influence on their development. Mentors must demonstrate equitable treatment of students when teaching and planning and not cause interns to prejudge students by giving them negative information about achievement, family background, or behavior. Interns will need advice on students and their background, but the timing, context, and tone of the information can have a dramatic impact on the intern's perception. It is important for the cooperating teacher to allow the intern to draw her own conclusions about students, but observations must be shared and clarification of perceptions discussed during formative conferences.

CHAPTER SUMMARY

Diverse classrooms can present challenges for student teachers. Opportunities to acquaint themselves with students, communities, and families help interns learn about the children they will teach. Monitoring instruction and interactions with students to ensure the intern is using equitable teaching practices, adapting instruction appropriately so all students can be successful, using a variety of teaching strategies, and making material meaningful for students, all provide the mentor and supervisor with data to foster professional growth of the intern. By observing and monitoring effective teaching behaviors in diverse classrooms, supervisors can ensure positive teaching experiences for interns in today's multicultural school settings. Table 6.3 provides observable teaching behaviors that can assist supervisors when working with student teachers. Finally, unknown bias—verbalized, implied, or demonstrated—by an educator is perhaps the most critical element impacting success in the diverse classrooms of today. Therefore, supervisors must pay significant attention to these behaviors during the student teaching experience.

Table 6.3. Observable Teaching Behaviors That Are Effective in Diverse Classrooms

The following suggestions were gathered by groups of mentor teachers working on a grant sponsored by the Kansas Department of Education at Emporia State University in July 2001.

1. Are student teachers adjusting lessons to meet the needs of students?
2. Are student teachers choosing materials for teaching that are appropriate to the interests and developmental levels of students?
3. Are student teachers varying their instructional strategies to meet the needs and developmental levels of students?
4. Are student teachers selecting varying assessments that meet the needs and developmental levels of students?
5. Do student teachers promote a nonthreatening classroom environment?
6. Do student teachers provide opportunities for all students to respond?
7. Do student teachers give positive reinforcement equitably to students?
8. Do cooperative learning groups encourage all students to work together?
9. Do student teachers adapt teaching and assessments to meet the needs of all students?
10. Do student teachers ask challenging questions of all students?
11. Do the student teachers' lesson plans reflect preparation to meet the needs of all students?
12. Do student teachers celebrate other cultures?
13. Do student teachers notice appropriate strategies the mentor teacher uses for working with diverse students and use them in their own teaching?
14. Do student teachers videotape the students while they are teaching to observe student behavior and involvement?
15. Are the grading procedures used by the student teacher fair?
16. Does the student teacher encourage the ESL student to teach him or her a few words of the student's own language?
17. Does the student teacher incorporate different multiple intelligence activities into · lesson planning?
18. What do students in the class say about the student teacher?
19. Read the student teachers' reflections to determine how they are viewing the students.
20. Do student teachers move around the room while teaching?
21. Does the student teacher communicate with parents and have communications translated into the parents' languages?

NOTES

1. Tara S. Azwell, Harvey C. Foyle, Lawrence Lyman, and Nancy L. Smith, *Constructing Curriculum in Context* (Dubuque, Iowa: Kendall-Hunt, 1999), 167–69.

2. Azwell et al., *Constructing Curriculum in Context*, 544.

3. Lawrence Lyman and Harvey Foyle, *Cooperative Grouping for Interactive Learning: Students, Teachers, and Administrators* (Washington, D.C.: National Education Association, 1990), 16–17.

4. Azwell et al., *Constructing Curriculum in Context*, 544.

5. Azwell et al., *Constructing Curriculum in Context*, 124–25.

6. Cathy Deschenes, David Ebeling, and Jeffrey Sprague, *Adapting Curriculum and Instruction in Inclusive Classrooms: A Teacher's Desk Reference* (Bloomington, Ind.: Center for School and Community Integration, Indiana University, 1999), 18–19.

7. Festus E. Obiakor, *The Eight-Step Multicultural Approach: Teaching and Learning with a Smile* (Dubuque, Iowa: Kendall/Hunt, 1994), 46–54.

8. Howard Gardner, *Frames of Mind: The Theory of Multiple Intelligences* (New York: Basic Books, 1983), 73–276.

9. Azwell et al., *Constructing Curriculum in Context*, 129.

10. Lawrence Lyman, Harvey C. Foyle, and Tara S. Azwell, *Cooperative Learning in the Elementary Classroom* (Washington, D.C.: National Education Association, 1993), 98–99.

11. Lisa Delpit, "Language Diversity and Learning" in *Beyond Heroes and Holidays*, ed. Enid Lee, Deborah Menkart, and Margo Okazawa-Rey (Washington, D.C.: Network of Educators on the Americas, 1998), 156–57.

12. Lyman et al., *Cooperative Learning in the Elementary Classroom*, 79–88.

13. Lyman et al., *Cooperative Learning in the Elementary Classroom*, 89–94.

14. William Stinson, Joella H. Mehroff, and Sandra A. Thies, *Quality Thematic Lesson Plans for Classroom Teachers: Movement Activities for Pre-K and Kindergarten* (Dubuque, Iowa: Kendall/Hunt, 1993); Azwell et al., *Constructing Curriculum in Context*, 128.

15. Harry K. Wong and Rosemary T. Wong, *How to Be an Effective Teacher the First Days of School* (Mountain View, Calif.: Harry K. Wong Publications, 1998), 176–77.

16. N. Zimpher and E. Ashburn, "Counteracting Parochialism in Teacher Candidates," in *Diversity in Teacher Education*, ed. M. Dilworth (San Francisco: Jossey-Bass, 1992), 40–62.

17. Ken Zeichner, Susan Melnick, and Mary Louise Gomez, *Currents of Reform in Pre-service Teacher Education* (New York: Teachers College Press, 1996), 109–76.

CHAPTER 7

The Incompetent Student Teacher

Working with a student teacher experiencing problems in the classroom is a concern of most supervisors. By identifying the cause of the incompetence and formulating appropriate plans for remediating the situation, supervisors can maximize the possibilities for success of student teachers who have difficulty meeting the expectations of their assignments.

WHAT IS AN INCOMPETENT STUDENT TEACHER?

An incompetent student teacher lacks skills and attitudes essential for success in the classroom. Most student teachers display some minor difficulties in one or two areas during the experience. These problems are usually easily remediated with normal supervision, and most interns are able to complete their assignments with success. Caruso outlines six stages of development for student teachers. Phase 2 of the stages is identified as confusion/clarity. In our experience, the excellent student teacher moves through all six stages very quickly, whereas the incompetent intern never passes the "confusion" of phase 2.[1]

However, a small percentage of student teachers do have problems so serious and detrimental that they are, in fact, incompetent. Because of poor planning, ineffective interpersonal skills, and poor management skills, student learning is negatively impacted by this type of educator. When dealing with an ineffective student teacher, supervisors need to assist the intern in solving the problems. However, it is important to remember that not all student teachers can or should be "saved," and that the failure of a student teacher who has received appropriate remediation is not the fault of the mentor or the university supervisor. Ultimate responsibility for success rests with the student teacher. This statement is very important to remember, since most cooperating teachers feel the failure of an intern is their fault. In cases where an intern's lack of ability is this severe, most mentors have spent countless hours working to improve an intern's performance. Unfortunately, some interns are unable to internalize and effectively put into practice recommendations made by supervisors.

It is difficult for a cooperating teacher to inform an intern who has invested considerable time, effort, and expense to become a teacher that she may not succeed in student teaching. Supervisors need to remember that their primary concern needs to be the learning and welfare of the intern's future students. With serious teacher shortages in the United States, it is possible that districts will be forced to hire less than ideal candidates to fill empty classrooms. The ongoing supervision during student teaching and recommendations of the supervisor are crucial in making sure that incompetent teachers do not become licensed teachers without first demonstrating the necessary skills and attitudes for success. A good question to ask when determining competence is, "Would I want this individual teaching my child or grandchild next year?"

Three general causes can be identified for student teacher incompetence. First, student teachers may be *unskilled*. Second, a student teacher may be *unaware*. Lastly, if efforts to remediate student teachers who are unskilled or unaware are unsuccessful, the student teacher may be *unable* or *unwilling* to work productively with students in the classroom as a teacher.

The Unskilled Student Teacher

It is common at the beginning of the student teaching experience for an intern to demonstrate less than proficient skills and abilities. After all, student teachers are in the mentor's classroom to acquire and enhance the skills needed for successful teaching. The difference between an unskilled and an incompetent student teacher involves a willingness to accept and implement recommendations for improvement. Usually, an improvement plan can be developed that assists the student teacher in acquiring the necessary skills to be successful.

When working with an unskilled intern, supervisors should provide examples from the intern's work that demonstrate a need for improvement and professional growth. If an intern is not dealing with student off-task behavior appropriately, specific examples of these behaviors should be identified. To make the intern aware that supervisors are concerned, examples should be discussed, and specific descriptions of the students' activities should be shared.

When working with an unskilled student teacher, it is usually helpful to address one area of concern at a time. By focusing on a single, specific area of concern, an intern can concentrate on efforts of improvement. It is easier for supervisors to give specific feedback when focusing on only one area of improvement. Also, if the student teacher experiences success in dealing with one area of concern, it becomes easier to target other areas because his confidence has been elevated.

Most unskilled student teachers are aware of their own shortcoming but do not know how to solve the problems. A helpful strategy in identifying solutions is to allow the intern to observe the mentor and look for specific ways in which she deals with similar classroom situations. Requiring taking notes while observing ensures that the intern is correctly identifying workable strategies that the mentor is using.

It may also be helpful for the intern to observe another teacher in the school who is very successful in working with problematic areas that have been identified. A conference with the teacher to be observed is not only courteous, professional practice but also allows the colleague to make sure strategies are demonstrated that would be helpful to the student teacher.

Another possibility is for the intern to observe the university supervisor or principal as he teaches a demonstration lesson with the students in the classroom. Many different approaches to teaching exist, and it will usually be helpful for the student teacher to become acquainted with a number of strategies to address specific problems or concerns.

After the student teacher has had the opportunity to watch other professionals, a plan for improvement should be developed. Together, supervisors should conference and ask the intern to identify those strategies observed during other classroom visits. The supervisors should also identify strategies that they believe would work well for the intern. After these steps, the supervisors should help the student teacher incorporate the strategies into planning and implementation.

When working with an unskilled student teacher, the number of formative conferences will increase. Although it is usually appropriate to have a brief formative conference at least once a week, a daily conference should be held while the student teacher is working on an improvement plan. Feedback should be specific and directed to the area of concern previously identified. Both supervisors need to note specific examples of progress and encourage the intern to continue utilizing strategies that are working well.

Unskilled student teachers need reassurance that all teachers struggle from time to time. Supervisors need to emphasize that teachers will encounter problems that need to be addressed through reflective practice throughout their careers. Student teachers should also be encouraged to seek assistance from colleagues throughout their career. Unfortunately, the truly incompetent student teacher usually is not aware of any shortcomings and often blames others. One common statement used is "They did not tell us or demonstrate that at the university." The blame may also be directed toward the attitudes of the children in the classroom or the cooperating teacher. Life situations such as family, work, or illness may also be offered as excuses. As the experience evolves, it will become apparent to both supervisors that the incompetent intern is playing the "blame game."

The Unaware Student Teacher

Student teachers may display incompetence without being aware that there is a problem. In response to clarification questions, for example, an intern may indicate that a lesson went well when, in fact, the mentor had several concerns about it. The student teacher may be in denial or really not know that something is wrong. Lack of awareness often manifests itself early in the experience and should be a red flag to supervisors. This type of intern should receive remediation early in the experience and a strong emphasis on students should be the focus of supervision.

Like the unskilled student teacher, those who are unaware need to be given specific examples of areas of concern. Awareness that a problem exists is increased when both supervisors refer to the standards reflected in procedures or evaluations. The mentor and university supervisor should compare the performance of and expectations for student teachers and make sure it is understood why improvement is needed.

The unaware intern may become defensive, suggesting that the areas of concern are not problems. For example, sometimes individuals will state that the teaching strategies they used are similar to the ones they experienced in elementary school. To counter this argument, supervisors should discuss the many changes in students, curriculum, and expectations for schooling that make different strategies necessary. Most interns, once aware that there are concerns about performance, are usually eager to improve. At this point, an intern usually exhibits the characteristics and attitudes of an unskilled student teacher, and procedures for assisting them are similar to those of the unskilled student teacher. Those techniques are observing others, addressing one concern at a time, offering specific feedback, and formulating an improvement plan.

Student teachers who are unaware they have problems may become unduly concerned about their progress when weaknesses are identified and discussed. Mentors and university supervisors should be positive and supportive during this initial phase. Noticing and commenting on specific improvements usually reassures and encourages the student teacher. Continued feedback, finding positive traits, and reflecting on one or two areas that still need improvement are key components when working with interns facing challenges.

The Unable or Unwilling Student Teacher

Although most problems experienced by student teachers can be remediated successfully using the processes described, a few will not be able to demonstrate the improvement required. In most cases, either they are unable to develop the appropriate skills needed or are unwilling to make necessary changes. It may be possible to help the unable or unwilling student teacher, but a great deal of effort is required to do so. When remediation efforts have been unsuccessful, the mentors need to communicate concerns to the university supervisor. If the supervisor has not already been involved in the improvement process, he must be included immediately. The earlier a university representative becomes a participant, the more likely all due process and appropriate procedures are followed. The mentor and supervisor need to work together to assist the intern. It may become necessary to eventually consider removing the student teacher from the assignment. If this occurs, procedures outlined by the university should take place. Treating this serious decision in the most professional manner ensures that all parties are treated fairly.

Discussing unsatisfactory performance with a challenging student teacher can be an unpleasant and stressful experience for both the cooperating teacher and university supervisor. Using positive confrontation strategies, however, can help make the task easier. Positive confrontation may seem to be a contradiction in terms, but effective supervisors can provide the necessary information an unwilling or unable student teacher needs to improve without creating unnecessary conflict. Although as educators we are concerned about an individual's self-esteem or "damaged eye," sometimes it is absolutely necessary to confront ineffective performers. It is an educator's professional obligation to do so; not confronting ineffective performance could be construed as malpractice.

There are six principles supervisors should follow when conducting conferences with an unwilling or unable student teacher. The mentor may find it difficult to apply these principles when conferences are conducted alone. The university supervisor should be available to participate in these conferences to minimize the stress for the mentor and ensure that all principles are appropriately applied.[2]

Conferences should have a positive tone.

Despite the unpleasant topics of discussion, supervisors need to reflect their concern and interest in the intern's success. Communicating throughout the conference that an intern's success is the primary goal of the triad enhances the opportunity for future implementation of a supervisor's recommendation.

Supervisors need to lead the conference and direct its outcome.

Unable and unwilling student teachers often try to avoid the unpleasant messages by distracting the supervisor or offering excuses.

The supervisor needs to ensure the conferences focus on key issues.

Key issues are the problems preventing the intern from being successful and may include a lack of skill, inappropriate behavior, or unacceptable attitudes. Again, the intern may try to direct the conference to less important topics, so the supervisor needs to make sure the focus of the conference remains on the important. Remembering to key in on two or three issues will focus and assist all involved in the conference.

Each conference should include appropriate and positive comments.

The student teacher needs to realize that the mentor and university supervisor are continuing to notice improved and appropriate teaching decisions, behaviors, and attitudes. An intern also needs to be encouraged when progress is made on an area of concern.

A plan of action for improvement must be developed during the conference.

The plan should identify specific areas of concern and detail how the student teacher is going to improve during the next teaching cycle. An appropriate plan might initially include a one week or so time frame so an intern can demonstrate growth in one or two identified areas of improvement. At the end of the predetermined time, the mentor, the university supervisor, and the student teacher will meet again to determine what progress, if any, has been made and decide the next step.

The conference needs to conclude with a summary of what has been discussed.

Supervisors should briefly summarize the concerns, the plan of action, and the time frame. Lopez-Real, Stimpson, and Bunton also identify six characteristics of a conference: identify the problem, understand the situation, provide support, discuss concrete incidents, trust the relationship, and be sensitive to the intern.[3]

DEALING WITH RESISTANCE FROM INCOMPETENT STUDENT TEACHERS

Since it is important for the supervisor to remain in control and direct the outcome of the conference, counterattempts by student teachers must be resisted. Student teachers may try to resist by using the following strategies:

- Refusing to acknowledge there is a problem
- Minimizing the seriousness of the problem
- Questioning the objectivity or skill of the supervisor
- Comparing themselves to others who "do it that way"
- Becoming defensive
- Becoming angry
- Blaming other people or circumstances

When the student teacher refuses to acknowledge that a problem or concern exists, the supervisor should restate the issue and provide appropriate examples. Reminding student teachers of expectations presented in university or evaluation documents may be helpful.

It is common for an unable or unwilling intern to recognize that a problem exists, but minimize the seriousness of it. The supervisor can counter this resistance by reiterating the concern and the triad's agreement. A supervisor can then identify why the problem is serious. For example, injury may occur if students are not managed appropriately. Identifying that students not treated in a fair and reasonable manner by an intern will affect the students' attitudes toward the subject and school and negatively impact learning.

When confronted, some interns react by questioning the skill or objectivity of the mentor. It is especially important that the university supervisor be present at these conferences to clarify that such criticism of a mentor is not appropriate. The intern should be refocused to deal with improving her own skills. If the student teacher continues to question the skill or objectivity of a supervisor, not responding to the intern's comments is essential. The cooperating teacher must remain focused on the concerns and redirect the conference in order to maintain a focus on issues related to the intern's performance. The supervisor can make a note that the intern raised concerns and possibly discuss them at a later meeting.

Some individuals respond to negative information by comparing themselves to others. Again, it may be helpful to remind a student teacher of performance expectations. It is seldom useful to compare one's performance with that of another teacher, and it is doubtful that an unable or unwilling student teacher can make such comparisons accurately. Therefore, it is usually best to redirect the conference away from comparisons.

Unfortunately, some student teachers respond to negative information by becoming defensive, hostile, or angry. It is sometimes effective to respond by describing the student teacher's behavior, for example, "You seem to be upset" or "You seem uneasy about our discussion." It is important that the mentor or university supervisor avoid escalating a negative situation by responding with defensiveness, hostility, or anger. If necessary, adjourning the conference until a time when the student teacher is more in control and less emotional may be best.

Another common reaction when receiving negative information is to blame other people or circumstances for the problems. If appropriate, the cooperating teacher or university supervisor can acknowledge challenges that the student teacher is facing. However, it is essential to redirect the conference and insist that the intern understand and assume responsibility for problems and continue to meet the expectations outlined by the supervisors.

There will be a few times when it is clear to the university supervisor that the placement in which the student teacher is working is not appropriate. It is the obligation of the university supervisor to ensure that the student teacher is given an opportunity for success and sometimes an assignment change can do this. There are times when the decision to make a new placement for a student teacher is necessary.

When a new placement occurs, the conditions for it must be clearly identified. Expectations for the student teacher should also be clear to all concerned parties before the placement begins. It is also useful to have an agreement or "contract" signed by the student teacher. The agreement should specify the conditions for and specify the requirements of the new placement that must be completed. The agreement may also identify consequences if the new placement is unsuccessful. For example, the intern may be required to wait a year before reapplying to student teach and, at that time, furnish evidence of successful experiences with students as a tutor or paraprofessional.

Finally, some interns "give up" when the problems being identified seem overwhelming. Supervisors should affirm their belief in the student teacher and their ability to correct the problem. In some situations, this affirming process may be difficult to express. If so, an honest and direct approach will better serve all parties. A realization by the intern that problems encountered in the current assignment are so substantive and possibilities for success are minimal must occur. At this time, a discussion about the possibility of removing the intern from the current assignment is necessary.

It is important that university policies for removing unsuccessful student teachers are publicized and known in advance by interns, cooperating teachers, and university supervisors. The university supervisor has a primary responsibility of protecting the due process rights of the student teacher and ensuring that policies are followed.

From the mentor's point of view, the primary responsibility must be to the students in his classroom. The desire to help a student teacher having difficulty cannot and should not be a detriment to the learning of students. As mentioned earlier, the mentor usually feels guilty when a student teacher does not experience success and is often willing to given an intern many second chances. Unfortunately, this can be at the expense of student learning. This must not and cannot be allowed to happen.

Mentors need to remember that it is the intern's primary responsibility to acquire skills necessary to be successful. By agreeing to work with an intern, a mentor provides only an opportunity for a successful, professional experience. Supervisors cannot guarantee the success of every student teacher.

FOLLOWING THROUGH WITH THE EVALUATION PROCESS

When plans for the improvement of a student teacher are made, the mentor teacher and supervisor need to follow up to determine if appropriate progress is occurring. Observational data from visits to the classroom, records of formative conferences, and documentation of the efforts made to assist the student teacher should be recorded and available if needed. If all of the conferences, feedback, reflective guidance, and specific examples of performance have not improved the intern's teaching, then both supervisors must be willing and able to inform the student teacher that she will not pass the internship.

CHAPTER SUMMARY

It is not unusual for an intern to experience a temporary lack of success in student teaching. Unskilled and unaware student teachers can usually improve when remediation and positive confrontation are used appropriately by supervisors. Student teachers who are unable to master needed skills or unwilling to change unproductive behaviors and attitudes provide a more difficult challenge. When working with an incompetent student teacher, the cooperating teacher should call on the university supervisor for assistance in conferencing with the student teacher. Together, supervisors should formulate appropriate improvement plans, monitor progress, and collect appropriate data to document the efforts made to assist in student teacher success.

NOTES

1. Joseph J. Caruso, "What Cooperating Teacher Case Studies Reveal about Their Phases of Development as Supervisors of Student Teachers," *European Journal of Teacher Education* 21, no. 1 (1998): 119–30.

2. Harvey C. Foyle, Lawrence Lyman, and Michael A. Morehead, *The Incompetent Student Teacher* (New York: Insight Media, 1992), videotape.

3. Francis Lopez-Real, Philip Stimpson, and David Bunton, "Supervisory Conferences: An Exploration of Some Difficult Topics," *Journal of Education for Teaching* 27, no. 2 (2001): 172.

CHAPTER 8

The Excellent Student Teacher

What characteristics identify the excellent student teacher? Some characteristics exhibited include the ability to learn quickly, good organizational skills, ambition, enthusiasm, effective use of varied instructional strategies, classroom "with-it-ness," relating well to others, and showing empathy for students. Other characteristics of the excellent student teacher can be found in table 8.1. This type of beginning educator, although perceived by others as a "high performer," will still need guidance and assistance. This chapter outlines a few examples of how a mentor might strategize while working with this "high performer." This chapter also provides examples of the professional conference, the reflective conference, and the motivational conference, and discusses techniques in conferencing that a cooperating teacher can utilize while working with the excellent student intern.[1]

Working with excellent student teachers, although very rewarding, may be as difficult as working with ineffective ones. Cooperating teachers may occasionally feel frustrated because they do not feel comfortable recommending ideas to superior performers. Nevertheless, outstanding interns need guidance and nurturing, similar to other successful professionals.

While working with excellent interns, mentors often encounter the problem of not offering enough specific feedback. Talvitie, Peltokallio, and Mannisto indicate that interns want more feedback than is typically given by mentors, especially early in the assignment.[2] A common statement often expressed by excellent student teachers is, "My cooperating teacher was great, but she never really offered any specific suggestions

Table 8.1.   Characteristics of an Excellent Student Teacher

This list is a composite of factors identified as contributing to an ideal student teacher from teachers attending the Cooperating Teacher Academy at Emporia State University from 1989 to 2000. They are clearly not in any order of importance. The mentor teacher may find it useful to highlight those qualities he thinks are of particular importance and share this information with the student teacher.

1. Conscientious	12. Caring
2. Prompt, punctual	13. Good planning skills
3. Flexible	14. Motivational
4. Cooperative	15. Problem solver
5. Accepts and acts on constructive criticism	16. Self-starter
6. Knowledgeable	17. Sense of humor
7. Honest	18. Wants to be there
8. Classroom management skills	19. Creative
9. Enthusiastic	20. Responsible
10. Positive attitude	21. Able to build rapport
11. Risk taker	22. Common sense

for improvement." Since outstanding interns are so talented, cooperating teachers often find it difficult to identify areas for improvement. In practice, however, supervisors must offer guidance that will enable interns to become well-rounded and complete professionals. Additionally, most outstanding student teachers desire to constantly improve; they want to be the best possible teacher. With updated methods of teacher and subject content changes, most classroom professionals are always learning and improving. It is necessary to include positive, constructive suggestions coupled with praise when working with this type of professional. It is important to remember that even the most capable beginning teacher can continue to improve and grow professionally.

If an intern is doing a sufficient job with the general day-to-day classroom instruction, a mentor should identify alternative areas for reflection and growth. Areas of growth may include, but are not limited to, new methods of instruction (e.g., cooperative learning), integrating technology (e.g., web quests), and academic content (e.g., updating the textbook). When working with this type of intern, a cooperating teacher can utilize the conferencing techniques mentioned earlier in the book, such as (1) questioning, (2) brainstorming, (3) clarification, and (4) reinforcement.

THE PROFESSIONAL CONFERENCE

Professionalism is demonstrated by maturity, self-direction, positive interpersonal relationships, a positive attitude toward other educators and a concern for the teaching profession. The professional conference between the cooperating teacher and the intern deals with interpersonal behaviors. For example, when an excellent student teacher does not exhibit appropriate professional relationships, he may demonstrate intolerance toward students or colleagues. Early in their careers, outstanding performers sometimes are not tolerant or understanding of others' life situations or professional circumstances.

An excellent student teacher who is outstanding in the classroom and has high expectations may not always exhibit appropriate understanding and patience in relationships with students or colleagues. One example is the intern who is not sympathetic to the life circumstances of students. Often, this behavior is exhibited by impatience with the student who does not put forth enough effort. Student teachers who are high achievers may not relate effectively to those students who cannot meet expectations. Most excellent interns are responsive to feedback, so a discussion about students with difficult life circumstances will most likely modify this behavior.

Additionally, early in some professionals' careers, rushing to judgment about other educators without understanding or knowing background information is common. In these situations, there are specific questions the cooperating teacher should reflect upon prior to meeting with the student teacher exhibiting these behaviors. The following questions can assist the mentor in preparing for the professional conference to discuss the lack of patience, tolerance, and understanding exhibited:

How do teachers exhibit behaviors that are perceived as unprofessional or uncaring? What types of circumstances cause outstanding professionals to become impatient with students and other professionals?

What would one say to a student teacher who exhibits impatience with students or other teachers?

In addition, the cooperating teacher may reflect upon how the conference should be carried out. The following approaches are suggested:

Reflect upon different ways to begin the conference; should it begin with a question, statement, or a description of the situation?

Together, decide ways in which an intern can deal directly with the situation and become more understanding.

Have the student teacher write a brief description of her perception about the student(s) or other professsional.[3]

Determine suggestions needed that would assist in identifying and changing behavior. Decide on only one or two specific classroom events or behaviors to discuss during the conference.

Share previous personal experiences that relate to the situation when appropriate.

THE REFLECTIVE CONFERENCE

The reflective conference deals with an intern who is always charging ahead and cannot wait for the next "new" opportunity. Becoming reflective is demonstrated by identifying personal strengths and weaknesses as they relate to teaching. Beginning teachers must practice the process of self-evaluation and self-improvement. The reflective conference is useful when meeting with this "thoroughbred" student teacher. This intern usually cannot wait for the next opportunity to teach and try new teaching strategies. Their minds work quickly, and they exude tremendous energy and confidence. However, sometimes an outstanding beginning professional tries too many different and innovative approaches without refining instruction and reflecting upon past successes. Prior to a reflective conference, the cooperating teacher might consider these questions:

What should the teacher say to an intern who is excellent in instructional methodology and always charging ahead with innovative ideas and techniques?

How does the cooperating teacher help an intern become more reflective about the educational profession and/or teaching?

Without dampening spirits, the mentor should assist in modifying these practices and emphasize ongoing reflection and instructional refinement. Some suggestions to consider prior to the reflective conference are offered here.

- Provide the excellent student teacher with specific examples for improving instruction. These examples could come from the cooperating teacher's experiences or observations of other teachers in the school building. For example, these experiences might include the latest instructional methods based on research and used in other classrooms.
- The cooperating teacher can provide specific examples of how she approaches improving, modifying, and implementing instruction. For example, this might include methods in which accreditation standards and state assessment practices are incorporated into daily classroom lessons.[4]
- Helping the student teacher reflect upon his experience is essential.[5] Providing personal approaches to conserving energy and eliciting reflection about teaching experiences are important supervisory responsibilities. In other words, the cooperating teacher might share how enthusiasm is moderated when preparing for the classroom so that clear comprehensive instruction can occur.

THE MOTIVATIONAL CONFERENCE

The motivating conference deals with the excellent student teacher who is hesitant to try new ideas and techniques. This particular student, although teaching effectively and perceived as excellent by others, is uneasy about exploring new strategies. Therefore, the cooperating teacher may need to use a more assertive approach. Because outstanding educators are always attempting to increase their proficiency, the motivational conference should guide an intern toward reaching her full potential.

The mentor has several issues to discuss with an excellent intern who is reluctant. The cooperating teacher can consider the following questions while developing a motivational conference.

How can one assist the intern in recognizing abilities not perceived?
How can one encourage the excellent student teacher to explore new
    areas?
How can videotaping or audiotaping instruction assist in the process
    of helping explore new teaching approaches?

Conferences with a hesitant student teacher should assist in recognizing good performance. The intern must be challenged to reach beyond
his comfort zone. During the motivational conference, consider other
questions that might help guide the cooperating teacher's discussion.

Is the cooperating teacher able to recognize when feedback is
    sought?
Does the cooperating teacher focus on one or two skills that encour-
    age risk taking? What are they?
How does one encourage another to embrace new challenges?
How does the student teacher exhibit reluctance to embrace new in-
    structional practices? How does the cooperating teacher cope with
    this resistance?

In addition to the above-mentioned ideas, several other conferencing
strategies can be used when meeting with outstanding student teachers.
These techniques include (1) developing questions, (2) brainstorming,
(3) clarification of statements, and (4) reinforcement of performance.
Although conferences with an excellent student teacher are not as difficult as conferences with an incompetent student teacher, they require
similar expertise in instructional and professional skills. The goal in
every case is to have the intern develop into the best possible professional. Reflecting upon the teaching process, expanding a personal
knowledge base, and having a vision for the classroom are important
areas of growth for all professionals and especially the excellent student teacher.

CHAPTER SUMMARY

When conferencing with an excellent student teacher, basic principles
to consider are: (1) everyone can improve professionally, (2) focus on

key skills, (3) encourage self-evaluation, (4) recognize professional ethics, and (5) deal directly with the issues at hand. These principles work especially well with excellent student teachers since they learn quickly, are well organized, are self-starting, demonstrate enthusiasm, vary instructional strategies, have classroom "with-it-ness," relate well with others, and show empathy for their students. Successful conferences will assist the intern in becoming more professional and reflective. Additionally, effective conferencing will assist in enhancing the professional development of the intern.

Cooperating teachers should not be intimidated by the abilities of outstanding student teachers. Mentors possess many skills, qualities, and expertise that can assist the excellent student teacher's professional growth. If an uncomfortable student teaching situation is encountered, the university supervisor can provide assistance, but working with an outstanding student teacher should be a very rewarding experience for all parties. Skills the cooperating teachers should assist the excellent student teacher in achieving and recognizing are:

Becoming reflective—demonstrated by identifying personal strengths and weaknesses as they relate to teaching. Beginning teachers must start practicing the process for self-evaluation, self-improvement, and reflection so they can become the best possible teacher.

Expanding the knowledge base—demonstrated by initiative, which leads to self-directed observation, questioning, and outside reading. The outstanding educator is always attempting to increase understanding of the teaching-learning process.

Creating a vision of their classroom—demonstrated by verbally describing and giving specific examples of the classroom environment, style of instruction, and desired student teacher interaction. Successful professionals are able to clearly verbalize a vision of their goals and professional environment.

The ultimate goal while working with the excellent student teacher is to develop a peer relationship—one that indicates to both parties that they view each other as equals in the profession. Justen and McJunkin discuss the nondirective approach to supervision and indicate the importance of trust and mutual respect. The nondirective approach in supervising will allow the excellent student teacher the necessary reflection time to develop this peer rleationship.[6]

NOTES

1. Harvey C. Foyle, Lawrence Lyman, and Michael A. Morehead, *The Excellent Student Teacher* (New York: Insight Media, 1992), videotape.

2. Ulla Talvitie, Liisa Peltokallio, and Paivi Mannisto, "Student Teachers' Views about Their Relationships with University Supervisors, Cooperating Teachers, and Peer Student Teachers," *Scandinavian Journal of Educational Research* 44, no. 1 (2000): 83.

3. Dian Yendol Silva, "Triad Journaling as a Tool for Reconceptualizing Supervision in the Professional Development School" (paper presented at the annual meeting of the American Educational Research Association, New Orleans, April 2000), 1–17.

4. Carman Giebelhaus and Connie Bowman, "Teaching Mentors: Is It Worth the Effort?" (paper presented at the annual meeting of the Association of Teacher Educators, Orlando, Fla., February 2000), 1–24.

5. D. Cruickshank, *Reflective Teaching: The Preparation of Students of Teaching* (Reston, Va.: Association of Teacher Educators, 1987).

6. Joseph E. Justen III and Mark McJunkin, "Supervisor Beliefs of Cooperating Teachers," *Teacher Educator* 34, no. 3 (Winter 1999): 179.

CHAPTER 9

The Principal's Role

As the primary instructional leader of the school, the principal should take an active role in working with student teachers. It is difficult for many principals to find the necessary time to play this active role because of the many other factors that compete for their time. In order to insure that student teachers are a positive addition to the school, however, the principal needs to be involved in decisions involving resources, selection, supervision, and evaluation of student teachers in his or her building. With the evolution of professional development schools (PDS) the principal's role is changing dramatically because of the need to collaborate in a more formal manner with teacher education programs. The proliferation of PDS's in the past decade has been significant, and the partnerships emerging because of the professional development schools movement have become more sophisticated and complex.

PRINCIPALS AND PROFESSIONAL DEVELOPMENT SCHOOLS

The National Council for the Accreditation of Teacher Education (NCATE) defines the PDS "as a learning centered community that supports the integrated learning and development of P–12 students, candidates and PDS partners through inquiry-based practice." In NCATE's discussion of PDS's they indicate that it is essential that there is a common vision and that the educational community support change and improvement in practice and in the partnering institutions.

The fall 2007 journal *School-University Partnerships* discusses numerous responsibilities undertaken by the principal. Gutierrez writes that a principal must be skilled in at least four areas.[1] First a principal's leadership has a significant impact on the success of a PDS. Second, a principal's knowledge of curriculum and their engagement in the assessment of instructional influence on curriculum implementation is another important skill needed. Third, principals must be creative at securing resources that include financial, human, and material. Fourth, the ability to actualize the partnership with the affiliated college or university is essential to the success of the PDS.[2]

Leadership can be accomplished in numerous ways, but our experience indicates that there are two key behaviors if a principal models it can insure a better chance for success of a PDS. The principal must model collaboration with the higher education institution. This modeling of collaboration sets the tone for other school personnel to follow and enhances the professional bonds developed between the two institutions. In addition, if the principal attends meetings involving the PDS, it demonstrates a commitment to the process. Although this is a simple representation of dedication, it is also a very profound statement on the part of the principal because of the time commitment required. It says to staff that the principal values the PDS enough to give of their valuable time.

The principal's knowledge of curriculum and instructional innovations is essential so the partnership with a teacher education program can be successful. The interactions between the principal, school personnel, and the university faculty will enhance the schools' access to knowledge of the new curriculum and instructional strategies emerging nationally. The collaboration whether through the PDS or through other partnerships will allow the school access to the most up-to-date curriculum and instructional strategies. The principal must take leadership in fostering a proper climate that allows the school to access the knowledge available through the partnership with the teacher education program. A principal's knowledge of curriculum and instruction strategies can be strongly enhanced by collaborative interactions and partnering with teacher education faculty.

A principal also must be a risk taker when it comes to the use of new instructional and curriculum programs. Because of access, both institutions can benefit from the partnership because teacher education faculty can study the impact of the new strategies and programs on teachers and students. As new ideas emerge, the principal must be knowledgeable enough to make informed decisions about new directions and opportunities.

The third skill needed to be a successful educational partner is securing financial and human resources. The mere nature of the PDS enhances resources available to the school. Often the issue of space in the early stages can create challenges for both the school and university, but once this is worked out, additional intellectual and academic resources are made available to the school in the form of students and faculty from the teacher education program. Ongoing planning with teachers and university staff can assist the school in providing additional services to students in the schools. Hermosa Heights Elementary School, which has been a PDS site for over ten years with New Mexico State University, is now provided services that include counseling interns and administrative interns. These additional resources provide assistance to students, teachers, and families that would not be available without the partnership.

As the PDS matures, the principal can work with the university to involve additional program support in terms of science experts, math experts, and social work specialists if the university has such programs. Additionally, university students and faculty can attend and participate in collaborative professional development programs that broaden the expertise of these individuals and therefore become resources for the students in the school.

Financial resources can also be enhanced, because foundations, state and national agencies often look for collaborative efforts to support. Professional development schools have an advantage when applying for grants because of the collaboration. University faculty are often expected to write for grants and have access to resources that can assist them in preparing the grant proposals. Also community agencies and companies are much more likely to offer financial support when the K–12 arena collaborates with teacher education.

The fourth criterion that Gutierrez outlines is the ability to actualize the partnership with the affiliated college or university.[3] Gutierrez goes on to say that the partnership should result in an energized and innovative environment.[4] This would be demonstrated by teachers, interns, and university faculty involved in a variety of instructional activities that would create a community that is reflective, innovative, creative, and often working as peers. A truly successful PDS might be one where an observer could not tell who was the intern, the master teacher, or university faculty member. The partnership can only be sustained through extensive collaboration and mutual respect. The principal can enhance the possibility of success by establishing leadership teams that are built around school-based issues and foster a reflective approach that honors all views and opinions.

BENEFITS OF STUDENT TEACHERS

Interns have many potential benefits for a school. Effective student teachers can be valuable additions to inclusive classrooms with diverse students whose varying needs require more time than the classroom teacher can provide. In effect, a competent student teacher helps to lower the pupil-teacher ratio in a given classroom. Student teachers also bring enthusiasm and idealism into the school setting. The fresh perspective of the competent student teacher is refreshing to both administrators and teachers.

In some cases, an intern brings new and updated methods of working with students into the school. When well prepared by the university, interns may have been introduced to new techniques and strategies that can be shared with teachers in cooperating teachers' schools. One area that significantly impacts schools today is second language learners and the tremendously ethnically diverse classrooms. Student teachers today are more aware of the needs of today's learners and are better prepared than students graduating ten years ago. Education programs today are much more sophisticated at preparing students for the diverse classrooms of today. In teacher education programs the growth of multicultural classes, second language learner programs, and the research of faculty in these areas has grown enormously during the past ten years. This type of new knowledge can assist a school when it sponsors a student teacher.

Having a student teacher in the classroom usually encourages the mentor to be more conscious of teaching decisions being made. Student teacher's questions may cause the mentor to be more reflective about why certain strategies are being used and how those strategies impact student learning and the classroom environment.

With student teachers come university supervisors who are usually willing to provide assistance to teachers in the school who are trying new strategies. University professors may be willing to practice and refine their own teaching skills by working in classrooms themselves.[5]

ALLOCATING RESOURCES

For a school that is not a PDS, resources necessary to support several student teachers can become somewhat of a challenge, especially if the school's budget is limited. But the benefits far outweigh the costs as one reflects on the advantages that interns can bring to a school.

While there are many potential benefits of having student teachers work in the school, the addition of extra people to a school takes resources which are often in short supply. For example, student teachers utilize parking spaces that may be limited. School staff may find the staff bathrooms and faculty lounge more crowded when student teachers are part of the school. The telephone may be unavailable because of necessary calls made by the student teacher or by those who work with student teachers.

Student teachers also use supplies, which may cause problems with limited budgets. While most of the supplies used by a student teacher are directly related to instruction of students, a generous mentor teacher may encourage the student teacher to duplicate his or her files for their own use. Student teachers may also find resources in the school media center that they want to duplicate. Principals need to determine whether this duplication is a benefit to the student teacher because of what he or she is contributing to the school, or if the student teacher should be expected to pay for copies made for his or her later professional use.

If the student teacher is using consumable supplies such as lamination film, computer supplies, construction paper, file folders, and the like to prepare materials for use while student teaching, few principals would reasonably expect the student teacher to pay for these supplies or to leave the completed instructional materials at the school when the student teacher leaves. The cost of such materials, however, may add up if too many student teachers come to the school.

Because the resources at most schools are limited, principals need to determine how many student teachers are appropriate for a given building. Policies regarding the use of supplies by student teachers need to be considered to assure that appropriate use is made of school supplies.

SELECTION OF MENTOR TEACHERS

Many universities ask for the input of the principal in determining which teachers are good candidates for mentor teachers. Principals should determine which teachers actually want to work with student teachers and which teachers are qualified to do so.

In general, mentor teachers should have a minimum of three years of experience. A mentor teacher should have demonstrated the ability to teach effectively and to relate well to colleagues in the school setting. The potential mentor should be knowledgeable about the content taught and about current strategies for teaching. Good classroom management skills and the ability to relate positively with students is a must for a mentor teacher.

Because of the potential benefits of having student teachers in the school, principals will occasionally agree to a student teacher placement without checking with the potential mentor teacher. The mentor teacher may have legitimate reasons for not wanting to work with a student teacher during a specific semester or year, and should always be consulted before the principal approves a student teaching placement.

Principals may also have requests for student teachers from teachers who the principal feels are not well suited to be a mentor teacher. It is possible for a teacher to be highly effective in working with students in his or her classroom and not be a good mentor teacher. We have observed over the years mentor teachers selected who are excellent teachers, but for some reason do not model the behavior that is needed for a beginning teacher. One example usually emerges related to planning. An instructor who has been teaching for several years might indicate to a student teacher that the extensive lesson plans expected by the university are not necessary. Extensive planning probably is not needed for that experienced teacher, but a novice teacher cannot plan enough.

These comments may undermine the expectations of the university and conflict with the expectations outlined to the intern. When this type of discord is fostered, it puts the student teacher in a difficult position and may encourage behavior that is ultimately detrimental to his or her success. This type of comment or attitude expressed by the mentor may set the student teacher up for limited success or failure and creates potential conflict between the university and mentor teacher.

Another example is the mentor teacher who does not give feedback and is unable or unwilling to offer corrective guidance when necessary. This teacher may be terrific with students, but with other adults he may have an aversion to offering feedback. This usually creates a climate of distrust and often leads to a student teacher receiving an evaluation she did not expect. Obviously this is unfair and often puts the university and school principal in a difficult position. In this case it is up to the university supervisor to ferret out the actual cause of the poor evaluation. This type of mentor teacher behavior can create tension between the parties involved and end in an unfair evaluation for the student teacher.

Professional development schools tend to alleviate these types of problems because of the extensive communication that exists between schools and teacher education programs. When the university approaches a principal with a request not to place a student teacher with a certain potential mentor, it does not mean that the university is saying that the teacher is ineffective or incompetent. These requests are made based on feedback from university supervisors and previous student teachers. The decision on the part of the university to deny a mentor teacher future students is done with the utmost care and deliberations. Although these decisions put stress on the relations, they are necessary. Requests to move a student teacher or not to place an intern with a particular mentor are typically caused by supervision approaches of the mentor and are not an evaluation or a critique of the mentor's teaching.

Student teachers have been placed in some classrooms because the principal feels that the mentor teacher needs help for one reason or another. The mentor teacher may, for example, be completing a graduate degree and need to have extra time to complete projects. A mentor teacher may be ill and need extra help and support to manage the rigors of the classroom.

Every student teacher needs to work with a mentor teacher who has the time and energy to supervise effectively. Principals should not make student teacher placements in classrooms where the mentor teacher is reluctant to have a student teacher or where the mentor teacher may not be able to supervise the student teacher appropriately.

The principal needs to meet with mentor teachers before student teachers arrive to make sure mentor teachers are aware of district and building policies which may affect their student teacher. Some of the issues to be clarified include:

When is it appropriate to leave the student teacher alone with students?

What is the policy for student teachers on reporting suspected child abuse?

How do student teachers turn in lesson plans when they assume teaching responsibilities?

How is the student teacher to be involved in staff meetings and inservices?

How are student teachers to be involved in supervision of students at recess and lunch?

How are student teachers to be involved in staff functions? If a social fee is collected from staff, is it reasonable to expect student teachers to pay all or part of this fee?

How are student teachers to be involved in accreditation processes for the school?

SELECTION OF STUDENT TEACHERS

Earlier, it was suggested that mentor teachers interview a potential student teacher before a placement is finalized. It is a good idea for the principal to sit in on these interviews if time permits. With many demands on the principal's time, it may not be possible to participate in each interview, but the principal should make sure he or she has met a potential student teacher before the placement is made.

MAKING STUDENT TEACHERS A PART OF THE SCHOOL

The principal can help to assure that every student teacher feels welcome in the school. The arrival of student teachers should be announced in the school bulletin. Student teachers should be introduced to the staff at a faculty meeting.

Parents and guardians also need to be informed when a student teacher will be working in their child's classroom. A note in the school newsletter can introduce student teachers to parents and guardians. The principal will also want to encourage the mentor teacher to send a note to parents and guardians letting them know about the student teacher's background and what his or her responsibilities will be in the classroom.

Principals will want to have an orientation meeting with the student teachers in the building early each semester. During this meeting, the principal will want to share basic information about the school and appropriate district and building policies. Some of the information for this meeting may be found in appendix 2.

SUPERVISION OF STUDENT TEACHERS

Although the primary responsibility for supervision of the student teacher is that of the mentor teacher and university supervisor, the principal will want to look over conference notes and lesson plans to determine how well student teachers are doing. Positive reinforcement, in person or in a note to the student teacher, lets the student teacher know that the principal is interested in the student teacher.

The principal should plan a formal classroom observation for each student teacher at least once during the student teacher's assignment. As an experienced supervisor, the principal can provide valuable feedback to the student teacher about his or her strengths and weaknesses in the classroom.

Some principals are willing to take the time to schedule mock interviews with student teachers. This is a real benefit to student teachers who are usually nervous about the interview process. By providing feedback to the student teacher about strong and weak points of the interview, the principal provides valuable assistance to the student teacher.

CHAPTER SUMMARY

The principal of the school where the student teacher is working has several responsibilities for the success of the student teacher. The principal needs to make sure that resources at the school are adequate for the number of student teachers placed at the school. The principal needs to make sure that mentor teachers are willing and qualified to work with a student teacher. By meeting with mentors and student teachers, the principal assures that expectations for student teachers are clear. By giving student teachers feedback on their teaching skills, the principal becomes an active participant in the student teacher's professional development.

NOTES

1. Cindy Gutierrez, Susan Field, Carole G. Basile, John Simmons, "Principals as Knowledge Managers: Helping Principals of Professional Development Schools Intentionally Utilize the Resources of the Partnership," in *School-University Partnerships: The Journal of the National Association for Professional Development Schools* 1, no. 2 (Fall 2007): 42–54.

2. Retrieved March 3, 2008, from NCATE Professional Development Schools homepage: www.ncate.org/public/pdswhat.asp?ch=133.

3. S. Bing and A. Goebel, "Using TK20 to Support PDS Communication and Assessment" (January 2008). Retrieved March 3, 2008, from National Association for Professional Development Schools PDS Partners online newsletter website: www.napds.org/Newsletters/NAPDS.

4. Lawrence Lyman, Alfred P. Wilson, C. Kent Garhart, Max O. Heim, and Wynona O. Winn, *Clinical Instruction and Supervision for Accountability*, 2nd ed. (Dubuque, Iowa: Kendall/Hunt, 1987), 4.

5. Lawrence Lyman, "A Professor Returns to the Classroom in a Professional Development School," in *ERIC Resources in Education*, Number ED439095 (August 2000).

Observable Instructional Behaviors to Reinforce

ANALYZING BEHAVIORS

1. The student teacher determines appropriate objectives for student learning.

   Observable behaviors:

   The student teacher communicates the objective of the lesson to students.

   The student teacher prepares course guides and materials that indicate appropriate objectives for student learning.

   The student teacher communicates objectives for learning to the mentor teacher and to the university supervisor.

2. The student teacher's instruction provides evidence of appropriate diagnosis of student learning needs.

   Observable behaviors:

   Students are working at activities at the appropriate levels of difficulty.

   Students are answering questions correctly.

   Students are expending effort to learn and are successful.

3. The student teacher's instruction shows evidence of appropriate analysis of the learning task.

   Observable behaviors:

   Learning tasks are sequenced appropriately to facilitate student understanding.

Adapted with permission from *Clinical Instruction and Supervision for Accountability*, 2nd ed., by Lawrence Lyman, Alfred P. Wilson, C. Kent Garhart, Max O. Heim, and Wynona O. Winn (Dubuque, Iowa: Kendall/Hunt, 1987).

The student teacher reteaches or moves ahead in the learning sequence as needed.

Transitions between learning activities are smooth and logical.

PRESCRIBING BEHAVIORS

1 The teacher groups students to facilitate student learning.
   Observable behaviors:
   A variety of instructional groupings are used.

   Student groups change as learning tasks change.

   Cooperative learning groups are used appropriately.

   The student teacher monitors groups while students work together.

   Students are on task during group activities.
2. The teacher facilitates critical thinking, creative thinking, and problem solving.
   Observable behaviors:
   Students are challenged to apply what is learned to their own lives.

   Students are required to compare, contrast, and categorize when appropriate.

   Student creativity is encouraged.

   Students are encouraged to support their ideas with evidence from their learning.
3. The student teacher relates learning activities to the objective.
   Observable behaviors:
   Connections between learning activities and objectives are clear.

   Appropriate review helps students understand how previous learning relates to a particular objective.

   The teacher paces instruction effectively.

DETERMINING STRATEGIES

1. The student teacher's lessons are structured to promote student understanding and remembering.
   Observable behaviors:

The student teacher presents information, gives directions, and responds to student questions clearly.

The student teacher uses effective examples.

The student teacher asks questions that promote student thought.

Appropriate wait time and prompts are used to encourage student involvement.

2. The student teacher motivates student involvement and interest.

Observable behaviors:

All students have the opportunity to experience success.

Students are actively engaged in learning.

The student teacher is positive and enthusiastic about students and what is being taught.

The student teacher emphasizes positive outcomes of learning.

The student teacher provides appropriate feedback to students about their learning.

3. The student teacher uses different multiple intelligence areas when teaching.

The student teacher uses varied instructional activities and strategies.

Observable behaviors:

Learning activities use oral language.

Critical thinking and problem solving are encouraged.

Music is appropriately integrated into instruction.

Pictures and other visual stimuli are appropriately used.

Movement opportunities are provided for students.

Students have the opportunity to work with others.

Students are encouraged to think about their own feelings and opinions about what is being learned.

4. The student teacher demonstrates effective classroom management.

Observable behaviors:

Expectations for behavior are clear to students.

Positive reinforcement encourages appropriate behavior and attitudes.

The student teacher responds appropriately to minor misbehavior.

The student teacher is aware of what students are doing during instruction and work periods.

LESSON DESIGN

1. The student teacher focuses students appropriately for instruction.
   Observable behaviors:
   The student teacher checks for student understanding of previously learned material.
   Smooth transitions are made from one activity to another.
   Student interest and attention are engaged.
2. The student teacher provides appropriate instruction to students.
   Observable behaviors:
   The student teacher provides appropriate input to students.
   Learning is modeled for students.
   Instruction proceeds at an appropriate pace.
   Appropriate closure is used to summarize the lesson before ending.
3. The student teacher checks for student understanding.
   Observable behaviors:
   The student teacher uses group responses from the students to check understanding.
   Appropriate signals, slates, or other strategies are used to measure the understanding of all students.
   Individual students are asked to respond to appropriate questions.
   The student teacher adjusts instruction based on student feedback.
4. The student teacher provides appropriate opportunities for students to practice new learning.
   Observable behaviors:
   The student teacher moves around the room checking student work and providing help as needed.
   The teacher provides answer keys so students can check their own progress when appropriate.
   Cooperative learning groups are appropriately used and monitored.
   Independent practice is assigned only after students have been successful in guided practice.

ASSESSMENT

1. The student teacher utilizes a variety of assessment strategies.
   Observable behavior:
   Students are provided with opportunities to create products that demonstrate their learning.
   Observation during in-class discussion and activities.
   Written feedback from students.
   Portfolios of student work.
   Pre-assessment compared to assessment after learning activities.

Professional Development School Agreement

The purpose of this agreement is to outline relevant policies and procedures for elementary professional development schools that provide clinical teaching experiences for university teacher education students in School District 000. All policies and agreements contained in the student teaching contract previously approved between the district and the university remain in effect.

INTERN RESPONSIBILITIES

Each intern who is assigned to a professional development school site will have met all requirements for admission to teacher education. Principals and staff members from PDS school sites will be invited to participate in the interview process for intern candidates, and the principal and mentor teacher have the right to approve all assignments of interns. The intern will provide the assigned school with a valid student teaching certificate issued by the university in compliance with the Department of Education and a valid health certificate completed in compliance with the Department of Health and Environment.

All interns are subject to university, teachers college, and department policies including the Policy on Student Ethics and Professionalism and Procedures of Due Process for Early Termination of an Off-Campus Teacher Education Assignment. Copies of these policies and other relevant information concerning interns can be found in the Professional Development Schools Procedures Book, which is provided to interns, mentor teachers, and principals at each PDS site.

PROFESSIONAL DEVELOPMENT SCHOOL COORDINATORS

A university staff member will be assigned as coordinator for each professional development school site. Coordinators will:

1. Clearly communicate program goals and objectives for the PDS to mentor teachers, building administrators, and district administrators
2. Clearly communicate PDS goals, objectives, and policies to interns
3. Clearly communicate time lines for required observations, presentations, and so on, to interns
4. Effectively coordinate the Teacher Education program outcomes
5. Effectively coordinate university faculty presentation schedules for interns
6. Effectively coordinate additional learning opportunities for interns
7. Observe and supervise interns during the first semester of their PDS experience
8. Observe and supervise interns during the student teaching semester, providing student teaching assessment and documentation
9. Conduct conferences with interns and mentors on a regular basis
10. Work effectively one-on-one to answer questions about individual interns and PDS goals and objectives

PRINCIPAL RESPONSIBILITIES

The principal of each professional development school site agrees to:

1. Assist in the selection of mentor teachers
2. Assist the coordinator by helping to clarify expectations for the professional development school with mentor teachers, staff, parents, and interns
3. Interpret school culture and expectations for the coordinator and interns

4. Observe interns as requested and provide feedback
5. Teach interns in areas of the principal's expertise
6. Serve as a liaison with central office staff
7. Assist in presentations about the PDS program as requested to a variety of audiences

MENTOR TEACHERS

Mentor teachers are recommended by the principal. Criteria should include: at least three years of successful teaching experience, evidence of ability to work with interns, and willingness to serve as a mentor teacher. A master's degree is preferred.

Mentor teachers will receive reimbursement for each intern who is placed in their class for at least sixteen weeks of the school year. The rate of payment is $_____ per intern at the time of this agreement. Payment will be made to the mentor teacher by the university after appropriate documentation as required by the state is provided by the mentor teacher.

Training sessions will be available to assist the mentor teacher. Reimbursement for attending training sessions at the time of this agreement is $_____ for a half-day session outside of the school contract time. Each mentor teacher is required to attend the mentor/intern meeting at the beginning of the intern's first semester assignment at the PDS site.

Responsibilities of mentor teachers:

1. Assist (as much as they wish to be involved) in the interviews of potential interns.
2. Help to develop initial training for interns, participate (as volunteers) in the delivery of awareness sessions and other training for interns.
3. Assist in developing a schedule for training mentor teachers.
4. Become familiar with the outcomes expected of students and suggest how these outcomes can best be met in professional development schools.
5. Assist in scheduling learning activities to assist interns in meeting expected outcomes.

6. Participate in training sessions for mentor teachers.
7. Model effective teaching for interns.
8. Explain reasons for teaching decisions to interns.
9. Engage interns in critical thinking to determine alternative strategies for accomplishing desired outcomes with elementary students.
10. Provide opportunities of increasing responsibility for working with individuals, small groups, and the whole class.
11. Assist interns in becoming self-assessing professionals who are ready to assume responsibilities for their own classroom.
12. Assist the coordinator in assessing the effectiveness of the professional development school and of the interns assigned to the mentor teacher.
14. Hold weekly conferences with the intern assigned to provide specific feedback on the intern's performance, reinforcement of areas of strength, and suggestions for improvement.
15. Demonstrate enthusiasm about teaching and learning.

Reviewed and approved on _____. Reviewed and approved on _____.

_____   _____
University Representative   Chair of EC/ETE
                                 School District Representative

Selected Bibliography

Abdal-Haqq, Ismat. *Voices of Caution: Equity Issues, Professional Development Schools: Weighing the Evidence*. Thousand Oaks, Calif.: Corwin Press, 1999.

Acheson, Keith A., and Meredith D. Gall. *Techniques in the Clinical Supervision of Teachers: Preservice and Inservice Applications*. 5th ed. Hoboken, N.J.: John Wiley & Sons, 2002.

American Association of Colleges for Teacher Education (AACTE). "Public Elementary and Secondary School Teachers, by Race/Ethnicity, 1993–1994 and 1999–2000 (in Percent)." U.S. Department of Education, National Center for Education Statistics Mini-Digest of Education Statistics, 2003. Retrieved February 3, 2008, from www.aacte.org/programs/multicultural/enrollment_ethnicity_yr93-94.aspx.

——. "SCDE Enrollments by Race and Ethnicity, 1989, 1991, 1995, and 2001." AACTE, *Survey of Teacher Education Enrollments by Race/Ethnicity and Gender, Fall 1989, 1991, and 1995*.

Anderson, Robert H., ed. *Clinical Supervision: Coaching for Higher Performance*. Lanham, Md.: Scarecrow Press, 1993.

Association of Teacher Educators. "Improve Recruitment and Selection." In *Restructuring the Education of Teachers: Report of the Commission on the Education of Teachers into the 21st Century*. Reston, Va.: Association of Teacher Educators, 1991.

Azwell, Tara S., Harvey C. Foyle, Lawrence Lyman, and Nancy L. Smith. *Constructing Curriculum in Context*. Dubuque, Iowa: Kendall/Hunt, 1999.

Bing, S., and A. Goebel. "Using TK20 to Support PDS Communication and Assessment." January 2008. Retrieved March 3, 2008, from National Association for Professional Development Schools PDS Partners online newsletter database website: www.napds.org/Newsletters/NAPDS.

Blackburn, B., C. Johnson-Taylor, and E. Young. "Effective Communication: The Key to a Successful Internship Experience." *Teachers as Leaders* 5, no. 1 (2004): 2–6.

Blanchard, Ken. *Whale Done! The Power of Positive Relationships*. New York: Simon and Schuster, 2002.

Byrd, D. M., and D. J. McIntyre, eds. *Research on Professional Development Schools: Teacher Education Yearbook VII*. Association of Teacher Educators. Thousand Oaks, Calif.: Corwin Press, 1999.

Campbell, Jane M. *Essentials of Clinical Supervision.* Hoboken, N.J.: John Wiley and Sons, 2005.

Caruso, Joseph J. "Cooperating Teacher and Student Teacher Phases of Development." *Young Children* 55, no. 1 (January 2000): 75–81.

——. "What Cooperating Teacher Case Studies Reveal about Their Phases of Development as Supervisors of Student Teachers." *European Journal of Teacher Education* 21, no. 1 (1998).

Charles, C. M. *Building Classroom Discipline from Models to Practice.* New York: Longman, 1989.

Clark, Richard W. *Effective Professional Development Schools.* San Francisco: Jossey-Bass, 1999.

Cooper, J. M. "Supervision in Teacher Education." *International Encyclopedia of Teaching and Teacher Education* (1995).

Costa, Arthur L., and Robert J. Garmston. *Cognitive Coaching: A Foundation for Renaissance Schools.* Norwood, Mass.: Christopher-Gordon, 1996.

Covey, Stephen R. *The 7 Habits of Highly Effective People.* New York: Simon and Schuster, 1989.

Cruickshank, D. *Reflective Teaching: The Preparation of Students of Teaching.* Reston, Va.: Association of Teacher Educators, 1987.

Darling-Hammond, Linda, and Joan Baratz-Snowden, eds. *A Good Teacher in Every Classroom: Preparing the Highly Qualified Teachers Our Children Deserve.* National Academy of Education. San Francisco: Jossey-Bass, 2005.

Davis, Bonnie M. *How to Coach Teachers Who Don't Think Like You: Using Literacy Strategies to Coach across Content Areas.* Thousand Oaks, Calif.: Corwin Press, 2007.

Delpit, Lisa. "Language Diversity and Learning." In *Beyond Heroes and Holidays*, edited by Enid Lee, Deborah Menkart, and Margo Okazawa-Rey. Washington, D.C.: Network of Educators on the Americas, 1998.

Deschenes, Cathy, David Ebeling, and Jeffrey Sprague. *Adapting Curriculum and Instruction in Inclusive Classrooms: A Teacher's Desk Reference.* Bloomington, Ind.: Center for School and Community Integration, Indiana University, 1999.

Foyle, Harvey C. *Clinical Supervision: A Cooperative Learning Approach.* Emporia, Kans.: Emporia State University Printing Service, 1992.

Foyle, Harvey C., and Lawrence Lyman. "Mentoring Your Future Colleagues." Paper presented at the fall National Social Science Association conference, October 2003, San Francisco.

Foyle, Harvey C., Lawrence Lyman, and Joanne Foyle. "Lessons Learned from a Culturally, Economically Diverse Classroom." Paper presented at the National Council for the Social Studies annual conference, November 1999, Orlando, Fla.

Foyle, Harvey C., Michael A. Morehead, and Lawrence Lyman. *Conferencing with Student Teachers: The Beginning Conference.* New York: Insight Media, 1992, videotape.

——. *The Excellent Student Teacher.* New York: Insight Media, 1992, videotape.

——. *The Incompetent Student Teacher.* New York: Insight Media, 1992, videotape.

Ganser, Tom. "The Contribution of Service as a Cooperating Teacher and Mentor Teacher to the Professional Development of Teachers." Paper presented at the annual meeting of the American Educational Research Association, Chicago, March 1997.

Gardner, Howard. *Frames of Mind: The Theory of Multiple Intelligences*. New York: Basic Books, 1983.

Garland, Colden, and Virginia Shippy. *Guiding Clinical Experiences: Effective Supervision in Teacher Education*. New York: Ablex, 1995.

Giebelhaus, Carman, and Connie Bowman. "Teaching Mentors: Is It Worth the Effort?" Paper presented at the annual meeting of the Association of Teacher Educators, Orlando, Fla., February 2000.

Glasser, William. *Choice Theory: A New Psychology of Personal Freedom*. New York: Harper Collins, 1998.

Glickman, C. D., S. P. Gordon, and J. M. Ross-Gordon. *SuperVision for Instructional Leadership: A Developmental Approach*. 7th ed. Boston: Allyn and Bacon, 2007.

Goleman, Daniel P. *Social Intelligence: The New Science of Human Relationships*. New York: Bantam Books, 2006.

Gordon, Stephen P., ed. *Standards for Instructional Supervision: Enhancing Teaching and Learning*. Larchmont, N.Y.: Eye on Education, 2005.

Gutierrez, Cindy, Susan Field, Carole G. Basile, and John Simmons. "Principals as Knowledge Managers: Helping Principals of Professional Development Schools Intentionally Utilize the Resources of the Partnership." In *School-University Partnerships: The Journal of the National Association for Professional Development Schools* 1, no. 2 (Fall 2007).

Hammond, Michelle. "Professional Development Schools: Synergy at Its Finest." *School-University Partnerships* 1, no. 2 (Fall 2007).

Henry, Marvin A., W. Wayne Beaseley, and Kenneth L. Brighton. *Supervising Student Teachers: The Professional Way*. 6th ed. Terre Haute, Ind.: Sycamore Press, 2002.

Hunter, Madeline, and Doug Russell. *Mastering Coaching and Supervision*. Thousand Oaks, Calif.: Sage Publications, 1989.

Jensen, Jacquelyn W. "Supervision rom Six Theoretical Framworks." Paper presented at the annual meeting of the American Educational Research Association, San Diego, April 1998.

Jones Institute for Educational Excellence. "Kansas Future Teacher Academy." Retrieved January 8, 2008, from www.emporia.edu/jones/kfta/index/htm.

Justen, Joseph E., III, and Mark McJunkin. "Supervisor Beliefs of Cooperating Teachers." *Teacher Educator* 34, no. 3 (Winter 1999).

Kopkowski, Cynthia. "My Debt, My Life." *NEA Today*, no. 26 (January 4, 2008).

Kouzes, James M., and Barry Z. Posner. *Credibility: How Leaders Gain and Loose It, Why People Demand It*. San Francisco: Jossey-Bass, 1993.

Levine, Arthur. *Educating School Teachers*. Washington, D.C.: The Education Schools Project, 2006.

Lopez-Real, Francis, Philip Stimpson, and David Bunton. "Supervisory Conferences: An Exploration of Some Difficult Topics." *Journal of Education for Teaching* 27, no. 2 (2001).

Lyman, L., F. Leone, and T. Delgado. "Strategies for Creating and Maintaining a Collaborative Community in a Professional Development School Setting." Paper presented at the annual conference of the Kansas University National Professional Development Schools, April 1997, Kansas City, Mo.

Lyman, L., L. A. Mann, and M. Patterson. "Community College Partnerships: Giving the BEST to Students." Paper presented at the National Social Science Association summer conference, August 2007, Vancouver, British Columbia.

Lyman, Lawrence. "A Professor Returns to the Classroom in a Professional Development School." ERIC Resources in Education. A paper presented at the national conference of the Kansas University Professional Development Schools Alliance, Kansas City, Mo., February 2000.

Lyman, Lawrence, and Harvey C. Foyle. *Cooperative Grouping for Interactive Learning: Students, Teachers, and Administrators.* Washington, D.C.: National Education Association, 1990.

——. "Creative Supervisory Conferences: New Wine in Old Skins?" *Florida ASCD Journal* (Fall 1989): 45–47.

——. "Facilitating Collaboration in Schools." *Teaching and Change* 5, no. 3–4 (1998): 312–39.

Lyman, Lawrence, Michael A. Morehead, and Harvey C. Foyle. "Building Teacher Trust in Supervision and Evaluation." *Illinois School Research and Development* 25, no. 2 (1989): 54–59.

Lyman, Lawrence, Alfred P. Wilson, C. Kent Garhart, Max O. Heim, and Wynona O. Winn. *Clinical Instruction and Supervision for Accountability.* 2nd ed. Dubuque, Iowa: Kendall/Hunt, 1987.

Mann, Lori A., and Lawrence Lyman. "Enhancing Public School and University Professional Development School Partnerships: The Community College Link." *School-University Partnerships* 1, no. 1 (Spring 2007).

McClure, Robert M. "School Improvement through Colleagueship and Cooperation." In *Cooperative Grouping for Interactive Learning: Students, Teachers, and Administrators,* edited by Lawrence Lyman and Harvey C. Foyle. Washington, D.C.: National Education Association, 1990.

Melser, N. A. "The Shared Supervision of Student Teachers: Leadership, Listening, and Lessons Learned." *Professional Educator* 26, no. 2 (2004): 31–37.

Miller, S., G. Duffy, J. Rohr, R. Gasparello, and S. Mercier. "Preparing Teachers for High-Poverty Schools." *Educational Leadership* 62, no. 8 (2005): 62–65.

Morehead, Michael A., Harvey C. Foyle, and Lawrence Lyman. *Conferences with Incompetent and Excellent Student Teachers.* DVD. Scotts Valley, Calif.: Create Space, 2003.

——. *Conferences with Student Teachers: Beginning/Ending and Formative Conferences.* DVD. Scotts Valley, Calif.: Create Space, 2003.

——. *Conferences with Student Teachers: Discussing Diversity Issues.* DVD. Scotts Valley, Calif.: Create Space, 2004.

——. "A Video Model for Conferencing with an Excellent Student Teacher." Paper presented at the Association of Teacher Educators annual conference, February 1989, at St. Louis.

——. "A Video Model for Training Cooperating Teachers in Conferencing Strategies." Paper presented at the Association of Teacher Educators annual conference, February 1988, San Diego.

Morehead, Michael A., Lawrence Lyman, and Scott Waters. "A Model for Improving Student Teaching Supervision." *Action in Teacher Education* 10, no. 1 (1988): 39–42.

Morehead, Michael A., and Scott Waters. "Enhancing Collegiality: A Model for Training Cooperating Teachers." *The Teacher Educator* 32, no. 2 (1987).

National Center for Education Statistics. "Minority Enrollment: Percentage Distribution of the Race/Ethnicity of Public School Students in Kindergarten through 12th Grade by Region: Fall 1972 and 2005." U.S. Department of Commerce, Census Bureau, Current Population Survey (CPS), October Supplement, 1972 and 2005. Retrieved February 3, 2008, from nces.ed.gov/programs/coe/2007/charts/charts05.asp.

———. "Projections of Education Statistics to 2016, Section 5. Elementary and Secondary Teachers: Introduction." Retrieved February 3, 2008, from nces.ed.gov/programs/projections/projections2016/sec5a.asp.

National Council for Accreditation of Teacher Education. *Standards for Professional Development Schools*. Washington, D.C.: National Council for Accreditation of Teacher Education, 2001.

Obiakor, Festus E. *The Eight-Step Multicultural Approach: Teaching and Learning with a Smile*. Dubuque, Iowa: Kendall/Hunt, 1994.

Pawlas, George E., and Peter F. Oliva. *Supervision for Today's Schools*. 8th ed. Hoboken, N.J.: John Wiley & Sons, 2007.

Renaissance Partnership Project. "Renaissance Teacher Work Samples." Retrieved January 14, 2008, from www.uni.edu/itq/RTWS/index/htm.

Roe, Betty D., Elinor P. Ross, and Sandra H. Smith. *Student Teaching and Field Experiences Handbook*. 6th ed. Upper Saddle River, N.J.: Prentice Hall, 2006.

Ross, D. L. "Cooperating Teachers Facilitating Reflective Practice for Student Teachers in a Professional Development School." *Education* 122, no. 4 (2002): 682–87.

Rubenstein, Grace. "Building a Better Teacher: Confronting the Crisis in Teacher Training." 2007. Retrieved January 8, 2008, from www.edutopia.org/node/4992/print.

Schwartz, Wendy. "The Impact of Professional Development Schools on the Education of Urban Students." 2001. Retrieved March 3, 2008, from ERIC Digest website: www.ericdigests.org/2001-2/urban.html.

Shulman, Judith H., Mistilina Sato, and Sharon Feiman-Nemser. *Mentoring Teachers toward Excellence: Supporting and Developing Highly Qualified Teachers*. San Francisco: Jossey-Bass, 2006.

Silva, Dian Yendol. "Triad Journaling as a Tool for Reconceptualizing Supervision in the Professional Development School." Paper presented at the annual meeting of the American Educational Research Association, New Orleans, April 2000.

Slick, Gloria Appelt. *Making the Difference for Teachers: The Field Experience in Actual Practice*. Thousand Oaks, Calif.: Corwin Press, 1995.

Slick, Susan K. "A University Supervisor Negotiates Territory and Status." *Journal of Teacher Education* 49, no. 4 (September–October 1998).

Stinson, William, Joella H. Mehroff, and Sandra A. Thies. *Quality Thematic Lesson Plans for Classroom Teachers: Movement Activities for Pre-K and Kindergarten*. Dubuque, Iowa: Kendall/Hunt, 1993.

Talvitie, Ulla, Liisa Peltokallio, and Paivi Mannisto. "Student Teachers' Views about Their Relationships with University Supervisors, Cooperating Teachers, and Peer Student Teachers." *Scandinavian Journal of Educational Research* 44, no. 1 (2000).

Teitel, Lee. *The Professional Development Schools Handbook: Starting, Sustaining, and Assessing Partnerships That Improve Student Learning*. Thousand Oaks, Calif.: Corwin Press, 2003.

Tharp, John M. *Breaking the Cycle of Failed School Reform: What Five Failed Reforms Tell Us*. Lanham, Md.: Rowman & Littlefield Education, 2007.

Vare, J. W., and E. A. Young. "Perceptions of the Quality of Mentor Teachers' Supervision in Professional Development School and Non-Professional Development School Settings." *School-University Partnerships* 1, no. 2 (2007): 9–18.

Voneschenbach, J. F., and W. B. Gile. "Dispositions for Teachers Education Candidates." *School-University Partnerships* 1, no. 1 (2007).

Wiles, Jon, and Joseph Bondi. *Supervision: A Guide to Practice*. 6th ed. Columbus, Ohio: Merrill, 2004.

Wong, Harry K., and Rosemary T. Wong. *How to Be an Effective Teacher the First Days of School*. Mountain View, Calif.: Harry K. Wong Publications, 1998.

Zeichner, Ken, and D. P. Liston. "Teaching Student Teachers to Reflect." *Harvard Educational Review* 57 (1987).

Zeichner, Ken, Susan Melnick, and Mary Louise Gomez. *Currents of Reform in Preservice Teacher Education*. New York: Teachers College Press, 1996.

Zimpher, N., and Ashburn, E. "Counteracting Parochialism in Teacher Candidates." In *Diversity in Teacher Education*, edited by M. Dilworth. San Francisco: Jossey-Bass, 1992.

Index